Ludvigsen Library Series

NOVI V-8
INDY CARS
1941 THROUGH 1965

Introduction by Andy Granatelli

Iconografix

Iconografix
PO Box 446
Hudson, Wisconsin 54016 USA

© 2001 by Ludvigsen Library Limited

All rights reserved. No part of this work may be reproduced or used in any form by any means... graphic, electronic, or mechanical, including photocopying, recording, taping, or any other information storage and retrieval system... without written permission of the publisher.

The information in this book is true and complete to the best of our knowledge. All recommendations are made without any guarantee on the part of the author or Publisher, who also disclaim any liability incurred in connection with the use of this data or specific details.

We acknowledge that certain words, such as model names and designations, mentioned herein are the property of the trademark holder. We use them for purposes of identification only. This is not an official publication.

Iconografix books are offered at a discount when sold in quantity for promotional use. Businesses or organizations seeking details should write to the Marketing Department, Iconografix, at the above address.

Library of Congress Card Number: 00-135942

ISBN 1-58388-037-2

01 02 03 04 05 06 07 5 4 3 2 1

Printed in China

Cover and book design by Shawn Glidden

Copy editing by Dylan Frautschi

Book Proposals

Iconografix is a publishing company specializing in books for transportation enthusiasts. We publish in a number of different areas, including Automobiles, Auto Racing, Buses, Construction Equipment, Emergency Equipment, Farming Equipment, Railroads & Trucks. The Iconografix imprint is constantly growing and expanding into new subject areas.

Authors, editors, and knowledgeable enthusiasts in the field of transportation history are invited to contact the Editorial Department at Iconografix, Inc., PO Box 446, Hudson, WI 54016.

Acknowledgments

The illustrations in this book are from the holdings of the Ludvigsen Library. They include not only a wide-ranging selection of photos of the great Novi racing cars at rest and in action, but also rare drawings of the first front-drive Novi and its engine provided by Leo Goossen to Karl Ludvigsen. Some of the car's predecessors are pictured to show how front-wheel drive began to set the standard for Indy cars and thus influenced the configuration of the original Novi.

Photos of the new rear-drive Novi at Indy in 1956 were taken by Fletcher Wilson. The photos of the Novi-Ferguson under construction in the English Midlands were taken by Edward Eves. Karl Ludvigsen and Stanley Rosenthall photographed it at the Speedway in 1964 and 1965. The fine cover photo of Jim Hurtubise in the Kurtis 500K-Novi at the Indy Speedway in 1965 is by Bob Tronolone.

Anyone writing about the Novis must refer to the two-volume history of the cars written with great love and enthusiasm by George Peters and Henry Greuter (Bar Jean Enterprises, Hazlewood, Missouri). Although not technically definitive, it tells the complete story of the racing career of the cars and the captioning is indebted to their *Novi–The Legendary Indianapolis Race Car* for much information.

The Ludvigsen Library and Karl Ludvigsen express their warm thanks to Andy Granatelli for his Introduction, which brings out dramatically the powerful appeal of these great cars to racing fans of those days and, indeed, forever.

THE NOVIS AND ME
by Andy Granatelli

When I came to Indy the first time in 1946 the track was mostly brick and weeds were growing in the corners. The grandstands were wooden shambles. And when a driver drove by, you knew who he was by the way he sat in the car and by the way he held his steering wheel. You could also tell by the way he bent over the wheel or how relaxed he was. You didn't need to see the car number. You didn't need to see anything but the driver. Rex Mays sat upright in the car like a giant. He sat with his arms straight out and he drove like nobody else could ever drive.

People have to have something to pull for. In the old days they could pull for the driver because they knew who he was by the way he looked, not because of a blurred car number. They pulled for the car because it was powered by an Offy, a Maserati, an Alfa Romeo, a Novi, a Miller, a Sparks, a Sampson, a Duesenberg, etc. Most every car chassis was different. There were 4-cylinders, 6-cylinders, 8-cylinders, 12-cylinders and 16-cylinders. There were supercharged and unsupercharged engines. Everybody had something to look forward to. It was very exciting and people came to Indy with their mouths hanging open like I did.

In 1946 Ralph Hepburn qualified and set a new track record of 133-plus miles an hour in the front-drive Novi. You might say, "133? That's no speed." Let me tell you something. The guys who first drove at Indy in 1909 were the greatest drivers that ever came here. Every year since the first 500-mile race, you had to be less brave to drive a car. The bravest driver was here on race one, day one, year one and so on down the line. Cars are so sophisticated these days that I could get into one of them and run over 200 miles an hour—no strain—because the cars support you as long as you have the driving ability. They go where you point 'em. But in those days they didn't do that. The cars had minds of their own.

So when I saw Hepburn qualify the Novi at 133.9 miles an hour... anybody who ever saw Ralph Hepburn drive... I can still see him right now coming out of Turn Four, and the front of the car was completely engulfed in blue and white smoke and the front tires smoking like they were on fire. When he stepped on the gas in the Novi a big blue-white cloud came off the front spinning and slipping wheels of the car. I can never forget it. And the sound of the car was unbelievable. I will never forget it!

In 1948 I wanted to drive the Novi so bad I could taste it. And when I told Ralph Hepburn that I thought I could drive the car, he said, "You could get 140 out of this. I'm an old man." He must have been at least 50 years old when he broke the track record. And, of course, I didn't drive it. If I had driven the car I'd be dead right now. I'd have been going 150 for one lap, for half a lap, for one corner. But it was a fantastic-sounding vehicle.

Like everyone else, I loved the Novi. Looking at the Novis, you were completely mesmerized. You'd just watch the Novis and you were hypnotized. You could listen to it idle there, just watch it and watch it. Everything else was nothing. When the Novi used to park in the garage area and Jean Marcenac would start it up, the crowd would get around it and be totally mesmerized. Mouths were open, tongues were hanging out looking at the car. That was also me.

When I used to own and run the Novis, people would write to me and say that they would literally get a furious headache from the car going by. Not that they didn't love the sound, but it would give them a terrible headache because they got so excited. Some people told me that they'd actually climax from the sound. That sound was something else, okay? ...something else.

Unfortunately, I ruined the sound. I'll tell you why. Before I owned the cars they sounded like nothing else you could ever hope to imagine. When there was one Novi on the track it would be heard over all other cars. It was the only car you could hear on the track, all around the track, when it qualified. Or when it was racing. You'd hear the Novi all the time. It didn't sound like anything else you could ever hope to hear. In order to raise the horsepower from 450 to 837, I reduced the size of the exhaust ports and headers. This reduced the sound from 150 decibels to about 125 decibels. Nevertheless, the Novi still sounded better than anything ever has, including today's engines.

In 1958 and 1959, before I owned the Novis, they didn't qualify because the hood used to blow off the car. The engine's intake manifold would explode and blow the hood off the car. Nobody knew what was wrong with it. Well, I'll tell you what was wrong with it …

In 1957 the car was at Monza and set a new track record there—177 miles an hour on the banked track—even through it was misfiring. This was the first time that the Novi could run with its engine wide open. So Jean Marcenac, the chief mechanic on the car, said to the Bosch people, "What do I need to make this car stop missing?" They said, "You need dual-ignition magnetos." So he installed twin Bosch magnetos with twin spark plugs. He had to design new cylinder blocks to put in new magnetos and twin plugs.

Now, this is the all-time classic. I bought the cars because they hadn't qualified in several years. I've always liked being the underdog. I always wanted to take something nobody else can do and say, "The hell with them. I can do it!" And I loved the Novis so much I think they're immortal.

So in 1961 I'm the new owner of the Novis and the engine's running on the dynamometer at about 3,000 rpm. I said to myself, "What's wrong with this engine? It's tearing itself apart inside." I couldn't stand it. I thought, "Jesus, this is not the Novi. Something is wrong with the engine." It was coming apart. I said, "Jean, what's wrong with the engine?" He said, "Nothing." I said, "Something is wrong with it. It's tearing itself apart like it has too much timing." He said, "Well, I put the timing in the engine. It's 25 degrees." I said, "Show me." So good old Jean—and there's nothing wrong with Jean Marcenac, by the way; the man has my undying respect forever—took the rotor off, took the cellophane from a cigarette pack and turned over the flywheel. He said, "See, it's 25 degrees advance, Andy."

I said, "Well, do you have a timing light?" He said, "No, I don't have one of those." I sent Ron Faulk back to Paxton in Santa Monica to get a timing light. And Ron came back and we put the timing light on it. The spark advance was 50 degrees, not 25. Normally, if you run an engine with 2 or 3 degrees more spark advance than it's supposed to have, it's going to burn up pistons. But to put in double the timing to 50 degrees is ridiculous!

The greatest thing I could ever say about the Novi engine is that it didn't burn up. It just exploded in the intake manifold because the intake valve was still open when it fired. It fired not only into the combustion chamber but also into the intake manifold simultaneously. So you had 60 pounds of pressure in the manifold which exploded the whole thing. The combustion chamber was also in fact the intake manifold and it exploded the whole engine. So I said to Jean, "Set the timing to zero." "Zero?" I said, "Yeah, set it to zero." He set it at zero and started it up and let it run. It had 25 degrees advance.

Jean had made a simple mistake. When the Germans asked, "How much timing do you run?" He said, "25 degrees." So the Germans put 25 degrees centrifugal advance in the magneto and assumed that Jean would set it at 0 degrees initial timing (in other words, top dead center). The ignition advance started out at zero and as you accelerated you got 25 degrees as a result of the centrifugal advance mechanism. So by *starting* out with a 25-degree initial advance he got double-timing.

Of course, when we put that right the engine started to hum again. We changed her in 1961 when I drove the car personally at 148.9 miles an hour. Dick Rathmann drove it: 149.7, 149.8, 149.9. The car ran like the champ it is. It sounded beautiful and everything else, but that's all because the timing had been double-advanced before. It was a simple mistake that resulted from the Germans not telling Jean that they'd incorporated the centrifugal advance in the ignition. But thank God for that. If he hadn't done that, I'd never have owned the cars and had all that beautiful heartache and you wouldn't be reading this now.

Although Harry Miller, at right, introduced his front-wheel-driven racing cars at Indianapolis in 1925, not until 1930 was a front-driven car victorious at Indy. In this Miller-Hartz, shown with owner Harry Hartz behind its wheel, Billy Arnold won the 1930 500-mile race. In 1932 Fred Frame won again with a similar Hartz entry, initiating an era in which front-wheel drive was seen as an avenue to success in this wealthy race.

The Novi of its day was the Miller-based Detroit Special, which first appeared at Indy in 1927. It had an unique front transaxle designed by Cornelius Van Ranst and two-stage centrifugal supercharging developed by General Electric's Dr. Sanford Moss, standing. Behind the wheel was famed driver Tommy Milton, who was closely associated with the car's construction.

As raced at Indy in 1929 the engine of the Detroit Special was equipped with this large intercooler, on the right-hand side, to cool the fresh charge entering the engine. Thin steel sheets in circular apertures were provided to be blown out if a backfire occurred within the intercooler.

Driven by Peter Kreis in the 1929 500-mile race, the Detroit Special developed some 300 horsepower. Said its designer, Cornelius Van Ranst, "White smoke poured off the front wheels on acceleration, in spite of more than 60 percent of the weight on the front. It would leave most other cars like they were tied."

In Indy racing history the V-8 engine configuration, chosen for the Novi, was extremely unusual. This was the partially dismantled 1½-liter V-8 engine of the Green Special that was entered at the Speedway in 1927 and 1928. Boosted by a Roots-type supercharger, it did not distinguish itself.

Most professional of the V-8 engines conceived for Speedway use was the 5-liter unit built to power the four-wheel-drive Miller of 1932, judged capable of 300 horsepower. Its cylinder banks were at a 45-degree included angle. Designers of this engine for Miller were Leo Goossen and Ev Stevenson.

In 1935, the year this beautifully streamlined Ford-powered Miller racing car and three sister cars were entered at Indianapolis, Lewis W. Welch left his Ford employment to become the owner of a company supplying parts to Ford based in Novi, Michigan. A Miller of this type was destined to form the foundation of the first Novi racing car.

All four of the Miller-built Fords that qualified for the 1935 Indy 500 retired with steering problems, including this one driven by Ted Horn. A front-driven chassis of this type acquired by Lew Welch and powered by a four-cylinder Offy engine finished sixth in the 1938 500-mile race.

Still with an Offy engine, Lew Welch entered his front-drive Ford chassis again in 1939 and 1940, gaining a third-place finish in the former year with Cliff Bergere as his driver. This was the unique Miller-designed transverse gearbox used in the Ford chassis—the chassis that would carry the first Novi V-8.

Married to the transmission of the first Novi-powered racer of 1941 was this compact flywheel. Machined integrally with it was the 55-tooth gear that drove the engine's overhead camshafts, supercharger and magneto.

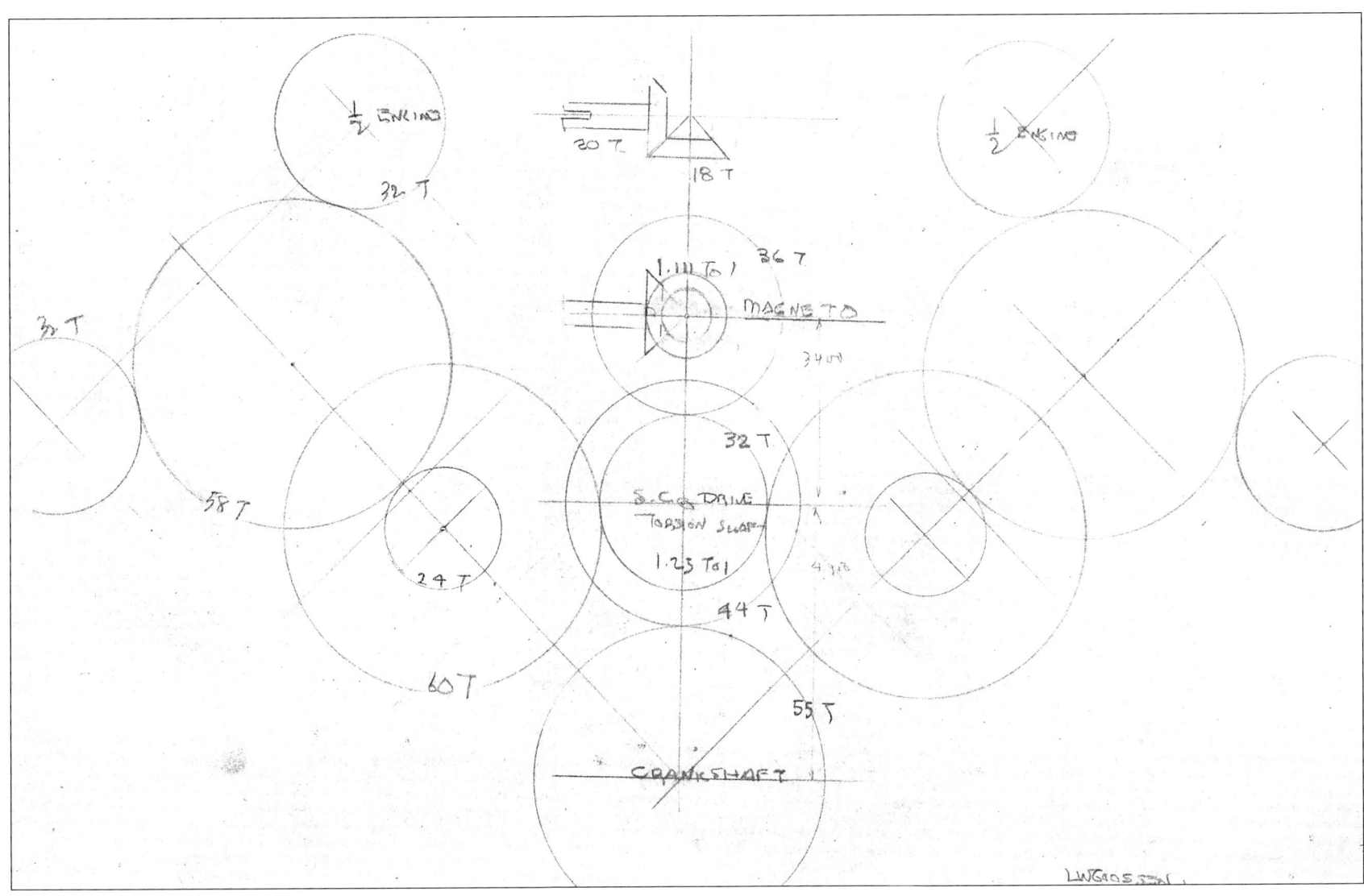

This original drawing by the designer of the Novi engine, Leo Goossen, showed the layout of its drive gears, which were positioned at the rear of the engine. The camshaft drove a compound gear from which the supercharger drive was taken. A bevel gear drove the magneto.

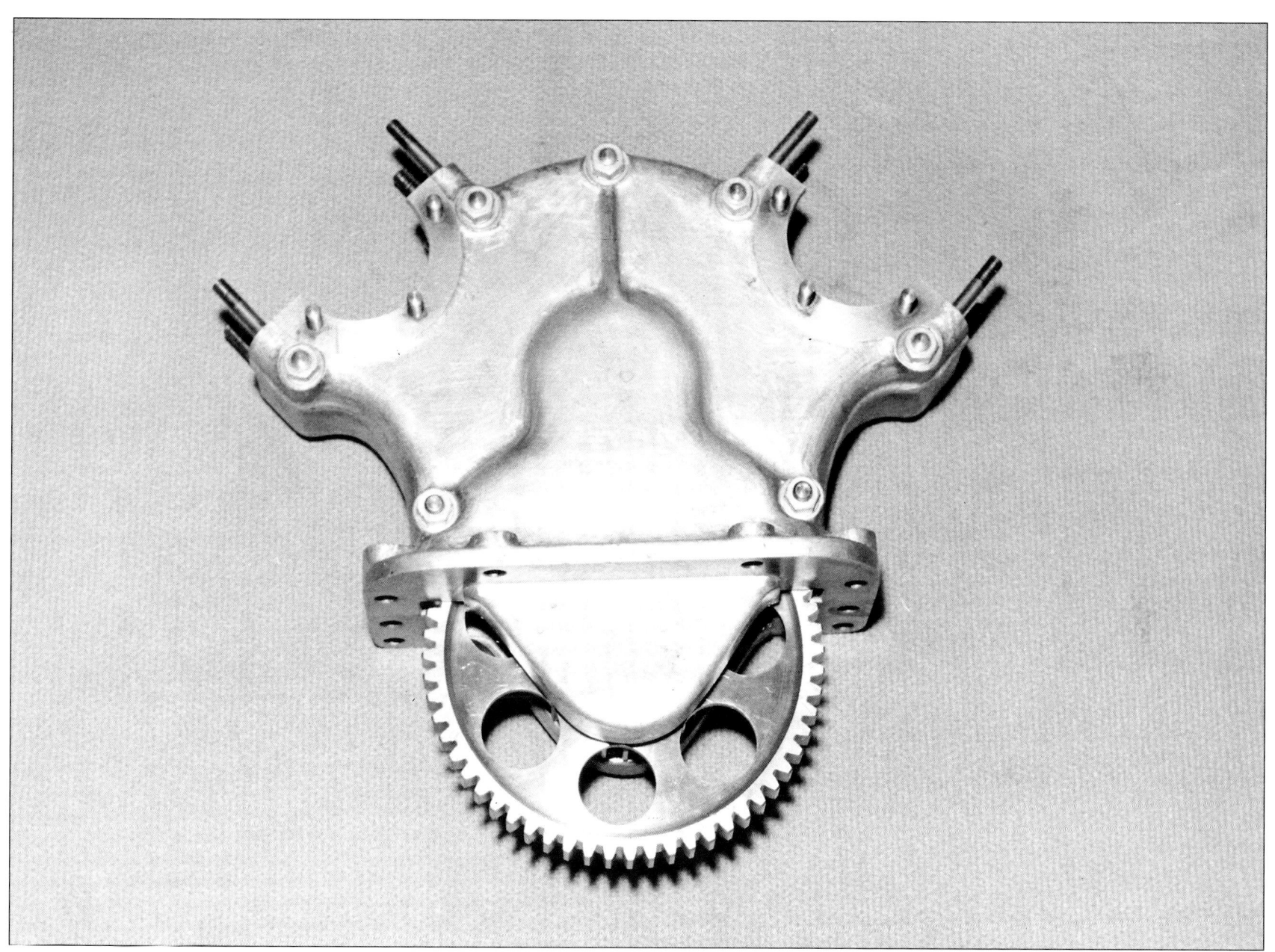
Each cylinder bank of the Novi V-8 had its own individual gear tower. The 60-tooth gear shown was driven from the central compound gear and carried the drive upward to turn the camshafts at half crankshaft speed.

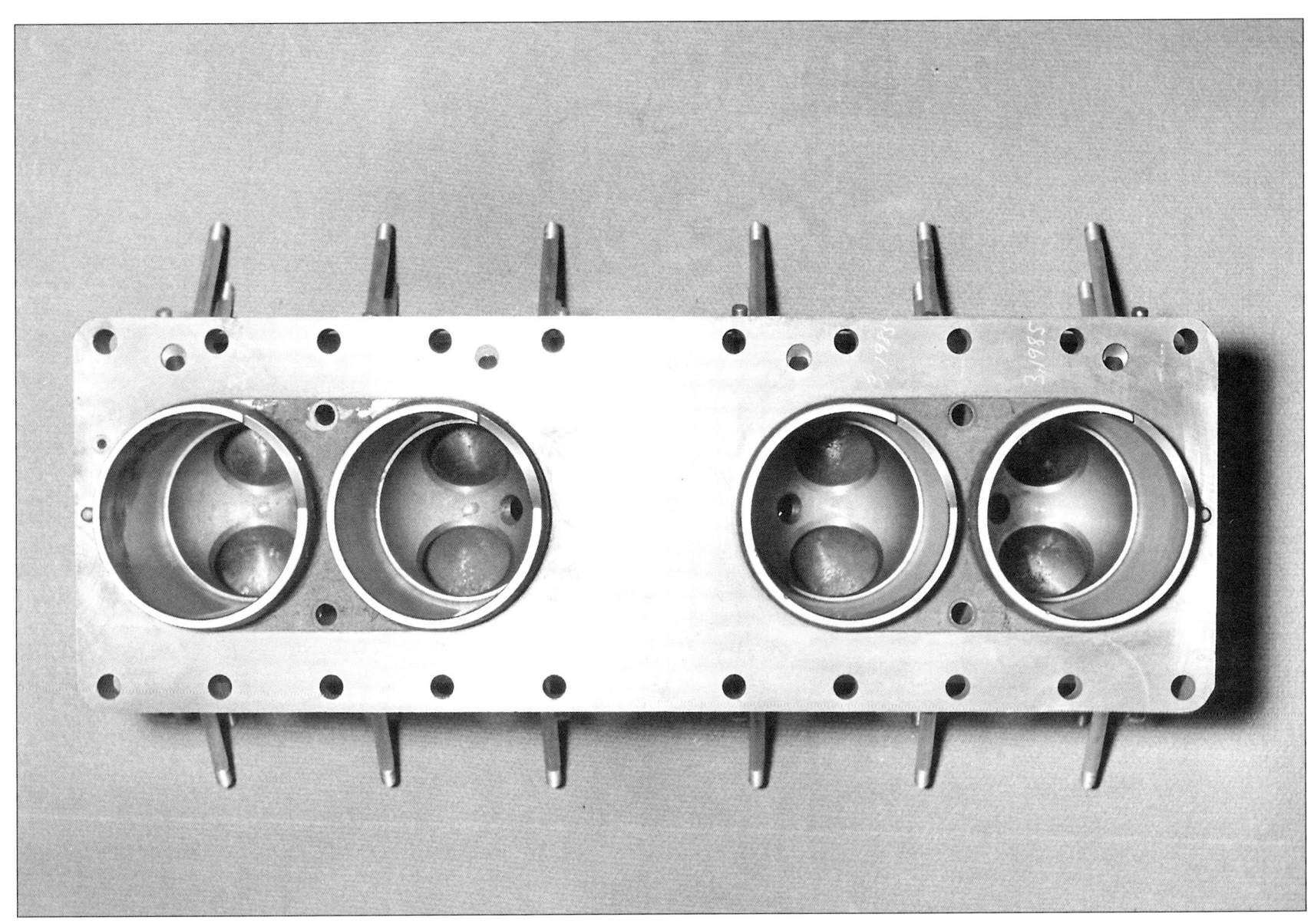

Miller design traditions were followed by Leo Goossen when he began work in a small Los Angeles pattern shop on the Novi's design in August 1940. Made of cast iron, each of the two cylinder blocks had hemispherical combustion chambers and cylinder heads integral with the block. Positioning of the spark plug away from the center of the chamber, as shown, was a change implemented in 1951.

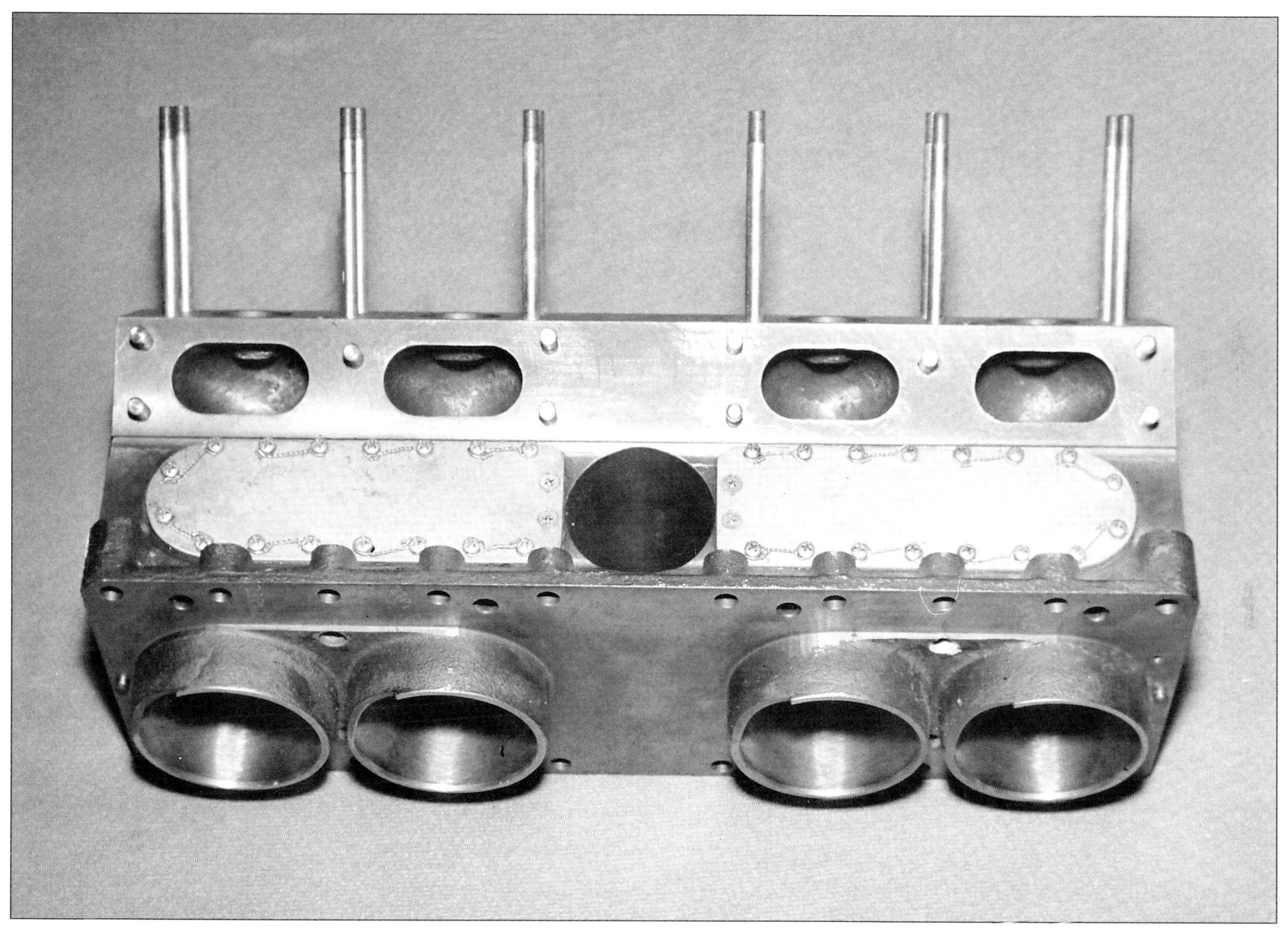

A side view of the Novi cylinder block showed the aluminum plates covering the access apertures to the water passages. These held the casting cores in place and allowed core sand to be fully removed. The central circular opening carried the incoming fuel/air charge from the supercharger to the intercooler.

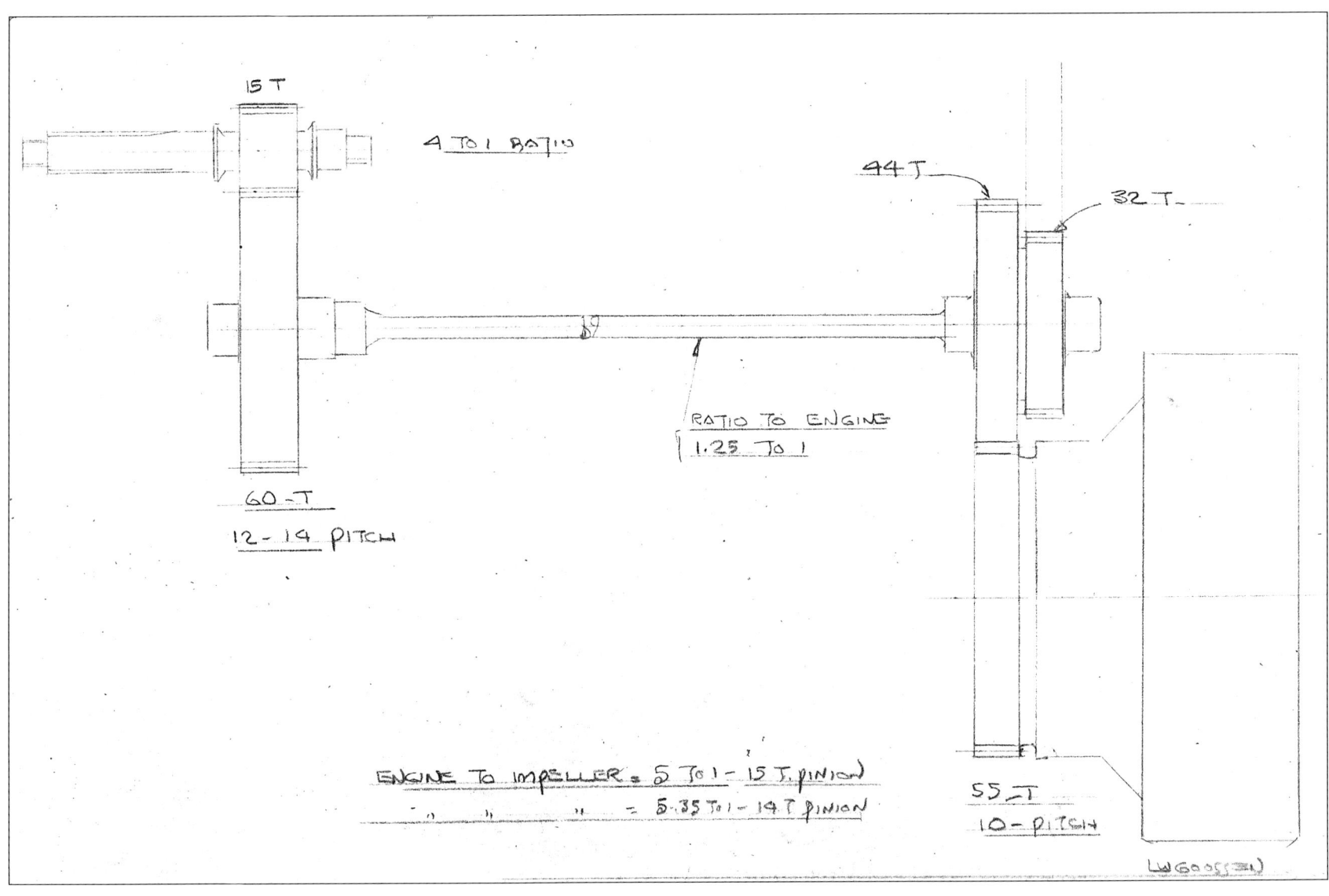

Leo Goossen's original drawing shows the way in which step-up gearing was arranged for the Novi's centrifugal supercharger. Goossen allowed for a choice of step-up ratios of 5.00 and 5.35:1. The long shaft driving the blower step-up gears was deliberately introduced as a torsional medium to cushion the drive. In Goossen's words, "This method relieved the gear train of shock loading caused by the excessive inertia loads of the impeller during engine acceleration and deceleration."

The centrifugal supercharger was mounted atop the crankcase at the front of the Novi engine. Although shown here as pointing upward, as it was in later installations, the blower's outlet flange originally pointed downward. As installed in a front-drive chassis the supercharger was naturally at the rear of the engine.

Installation of the new V-8 engine in the Ford chassis for the 1941 race showed the design of its top-mounted intercooler. Pressure fuel/air mixture came up from the center of the unit to pass through the intercooler, which received cooling air through a duct from the nose. Induction air under pressure then passed out to the sides and down into the inlet manifolds, which were equipped with spring-loaded pressure-relief valves. The two water exits from each cylinder head were kept small to create internal pressure in the blocks, a characteristic of Miller design.

Looking over their new creation in 1941 were Goossen, left, Fred Offenhauser, whose shop made the engine and, right, Bud Winfield, who developed the engine's concept for Lew Welch and was the team's chief mechanic. Three of Winfield's brother Ed's racing carburetors fed the supercharger of an engine that was initially known as a "Winfield V-8."

To drive his new 1941 racing car Welch chose Ralph Hepburn, an Indy Speedway veteran who had experience of the front-drive supercharged Millers of the late 1920s. Hepburn was not impressed by the car's handling, with its 450 horsepower in a chassis originally designed to cope with a modified Ford V-8 delivering little more than 160 bhp.

Posing with his 1941 Indy entry was Lew Welch, at center, with mechanic "Radio" Gardner on his right and the tall Bud Winfield on his left. Ralph Hepburn shrewdly limited the engine's throttle travel to be able to drive the powerful chassis to a fourth-place finish. He made only two pit stops during his steady drive.

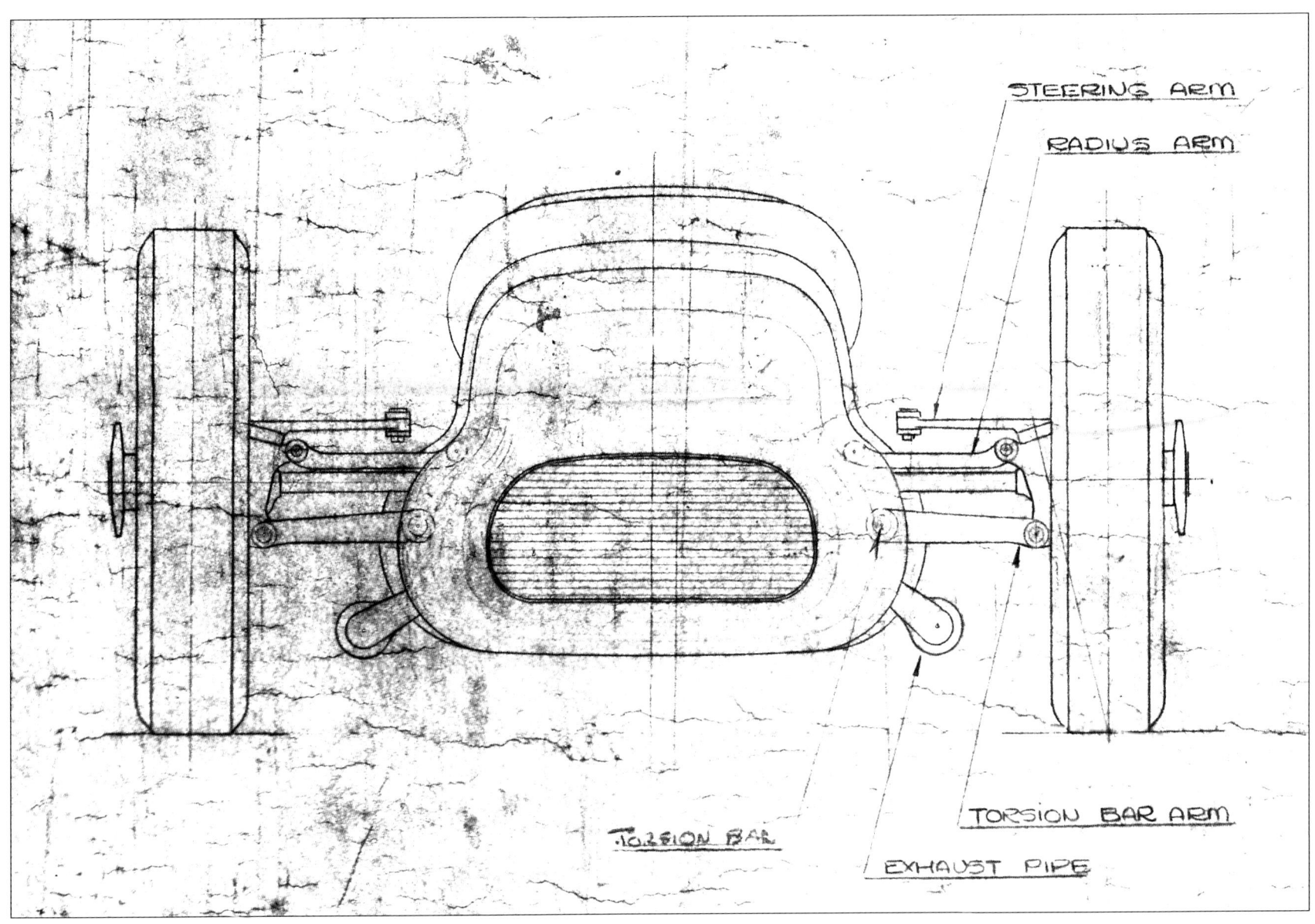

For Bud Winfield's company, which supervised the work on behalf of Lew Welch, Leo Goossen began work in August 1945 on the design of a completely new car to house the engine that would become known as the Novi V-8. In his

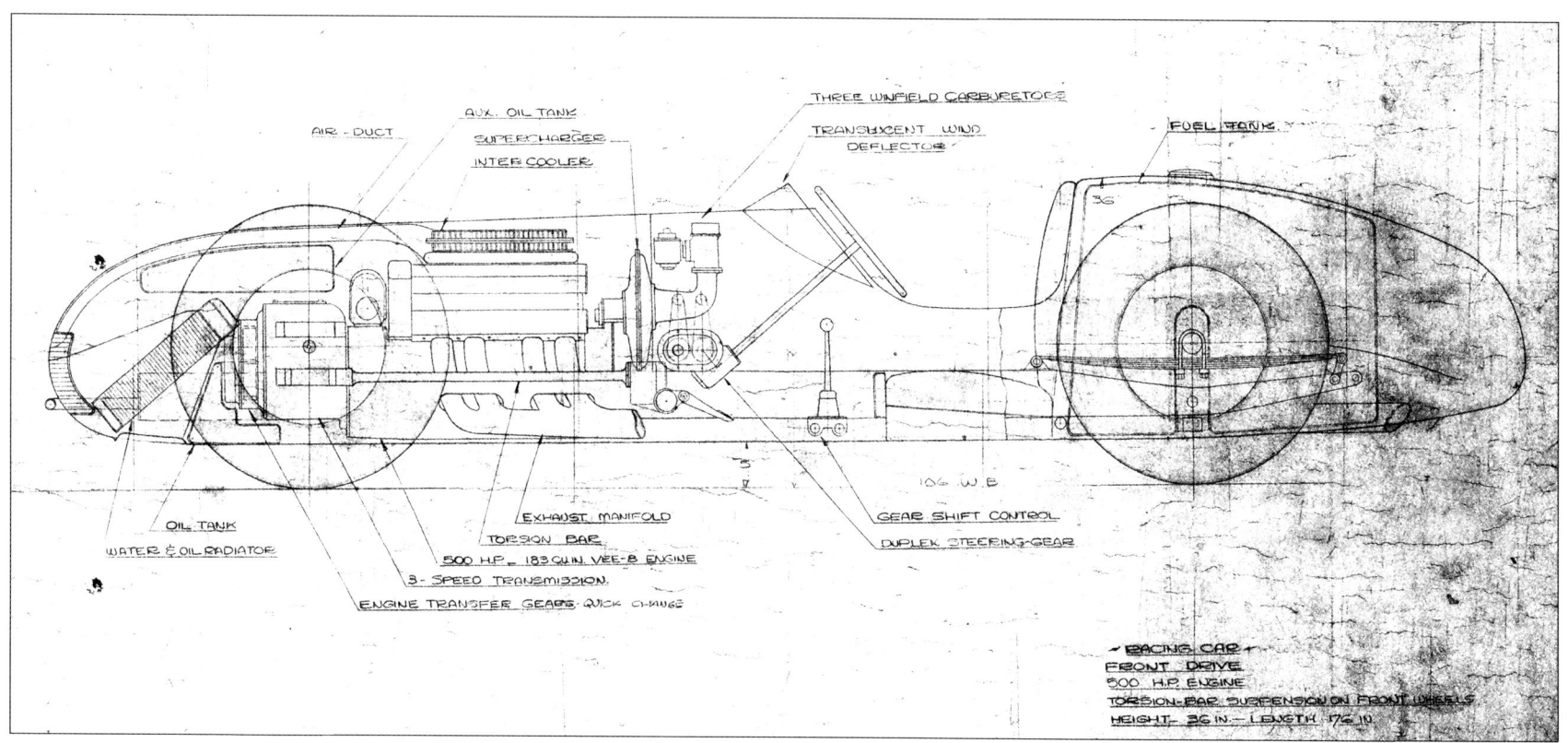

overall layout drawing, completed on March 22, 1946, Goossen showed the new car's 106-inch wheelbase and low build. Front wheels were sprung independently by torsion bars and the solid rear axle was carried by semi-elliptic springs. Quick-change transfer gears were designed into the front of the new three-speed transmission. Goossen took care to have the axis of the front steering knuckle pass through the center of the contact patch between the front wheel and the pavement. This was seen at the time as an important characteristic of a front-driven racing car.

A comparison showed the piston and connecting rod of the 3-liter Novi, right, in relation to the rod and piston of the 4½-liter four-cylinder Offy engine, left. The initial dimensions of the Novi cylinder were 3.125 x 2.937 inches (79.4 x 76.6mm).

To Leo Goossen's design, overseen by Bud Winfield, the first of the new Novi racing cars was built in the Glendale, California shop of Frank Kurtis early in 1946. Driver Ralph Hepburn looked on as Lew Welch attended to some details of the impressive machine. The duct over the radiator carried air to the engine's intercooler.

Although it arrived late at the Speedway in 1946, the new Novi Governor Special (Welch produced engine governors) soon showed its paces. On the last day of qualifying Hepburn turned four laps at an average of 133.944 mph, 3.8 mph faster than the previous qualifying record set in 1939. Although starting 19th, Hepburn was immediately among the favorites for the race.

In his long, low and gorgeous blue Novi, Hepburn took the lead in the 1946 race on the 12th lap after setting a lap record of 129.9 mph. He was delayed by attention to the brakes, however, and finally retired with engine failure after 121 of the 200 laps. By any standards, however, the fast and glamorous Novi was Indy's new sensation.

For the 1947 Indy 500-mile race a second Novi was built at the Kurtis shop. Bud Winfield looked a happy man behind the wheel of one of the two 1947 entries. The Indianapolis Speedway's famous pagoda is visible in the background.

Lew Welch, left, coached Jimmy Jackson, one of the potential drivers of the Novis in 1947. Cliff Bergere qualified his Novi in the center of the front row and after his own mount failed he took over the sister car of Herb Ardinger to finish fourth. Heavy wear of the front tires of a hard-driven Novi was a handicap for these very fast cars.

Powered by the Meyer-Drake Offy four, Lou Moore's Blue Crown Specials served as convincing advocates for the merits of front-wheel drive at the Indy Speedway. Seen from the right side of the engine room, the Blue Crowns were laid out much like the Novis with a three-speed transaxle and quick-change gears placed forward of the engine.

Running with impressive economy on gasoline instead of methanol, the Blue Crowns were the Indy 500 winners in 1947, 1948 and 1949. Mauri Rose, nearest the camera, was the 1947 winner. He shared the front row that year with Cliff Bergere's Novi, in the center, and the supercharged 3-liter 8-cylinder Maserati of Ted Horn.

The Frank Kurtis shop built a special canopy and tail covering for a Novi that was taken to the Bonneville Salt Flats for record-breaking attempts in 1947. Although the initial idea was to attempt a new record for 24 hours, this was given up when veteran record-breaker Ab Jenkins said he was not comfortable in the car.

During record attempts at Bonneville, Novi owner Lew Welch had a chance to drive his car, the newer of the two racers built. Welch was said to have reached some 170 mph on the salt surface.

In the waning evening light of August 21, 1947, Ab Jenkins' son Marvin made runs in two directions on a circular track at Bonneville. His average of 179.434 mph broke an International Class D record and a number of U.S.

National records as well. He was timed in one direction at 183.6 mph in a run that included a spell at more than 200 mph. This image shows the car during tests at Muroc Dry Lake.

Arriving in the Speedway's "Gasoline Alley" in 1948 the Novis were seen to be all cream instead of the cream and red 1947 scheme. Lew Welch and a pipe-smoking Bud Winfield supervised from the truck while driver Cliff Bergere handled the left front tire. For 1948 the Novi's tank was enlarged from 85 to the remarkable capacity of 112 gallons—weighing 670 pounds—to allow it to travel farther on its methanol fuel.

New to the Novi team in 1948, Duke Nalon was that year's fastest qualifier at an average 131.603 mph. Nalon was often in contention for the lead, but at his mid-race pit stop his crew failed to fill the tank and he had to stop on lap 186 for additional fuel. He nevertheless placed third, the best finish a Novi was ever to enjoy at Indianapolis.

Tragedy struck the Novi team in 1948. The popular Ralph Hepburn was killed when his Novi went out of control and hit the wall head on. The 52-year-old driver died instantly from severe head and chest injuries. The Novi began to gain a reputation as a car that needed watching.

For the 1949 race Bud Winfield arranged straps at the sides of the intercooler to hold it to the manifold below. Some suspicion had arisen in 1948 that Duke Nalon's shortage of fuel during the race might have been owed to a lifting of the intercooler and a consequent opening of the hose connections between it and the inlet manifolds.

For the 1949 Indy 500 Welch and Winfield assembled an outstanding driving team in Dennis "Duke" Nalon and racing star Rex Mays, who had qualified four times for the Indy pole. Mechanic "Radio" Gardner posed with one of the cars and a representative of sponsor Mobil.

Rex Mays, shown, qualified in 1949 at 129.552 mph against the speed of 132.939 mph of polesitter Nalon. While Mays retired on lap 48 with a magneto failure, Nalon crashed on lap 23 after his rear axle broke and the left rear wheel came adrift. Nalon was lucky to escape from his wrecked and flaming Novi.

In 1950 the Novis, newly equipped with a Holley aircraft carburetor, failed to qualify. In 1951, however, Duke Nalon set a new qualifying four-lap record at 136.498 mph with a best lap of 137.049. Visible on the car's cowl was the new air inlet for the Holley. Behind Nalon was a new 1951 Chrysler with its soon-to-be-famous "Hemi" V-8.

Unsurprisingly, polesitter Nalon and his Novi attracted the attention of Speedway notables. Benson Ford of the Ford family was nearest the driver talking with Speedway General Manager Wilbur Shaw, himself a three-time winner of the race. Pure Oil was the team's sponsor in 1951.

Although a late qualifier, as was often the case with the Novis, in 1951 Indy veteran Chet Miller qualified on the final day at the excellent average of 135.798 mph with a quickest lap of 137.615 mph. Only one faster single lap had ever been officially timed at the Speedway. In the race Miller was slowed by ignition and tire problems.

Bogged down behind a slowcoach of a pace-car driver, the cream Novi of Duke Nalon fell from pole position to fourth on the inside of the first turn. Following many pit stops and various vicissitudes the Novi stopped on lap 151. Such was the attrition in 1951 that Nalon was still classified tenth.

Ever the optimist, Lew Welch, in cap, increased the boost and power of his Novis for the 1952 race. Newly in charge of mechanical work on the cars was French-born Jean Marcenac, who had joined the Welch stable when a second car was added in 1947. Born in 1895, Marcenac had originally come to Indy with the Ballot team in 1920. Later settling in America, Marcenac was the crew chief for the Indy winners of 1927, 1929, 1930 and 1932. He took over technical responsibility for the Novis after Bud Winfield's death in a road accident in November 1950.

During practice in 1952 Chet Miller lapped the Speedway at 140.87 mph, suggesting that great things were to come. His four-lap qualifying average of 139.034 mph was a new record. Both cars were out before the race's halfway mark, however, with failure of the supercharger drive shafts.

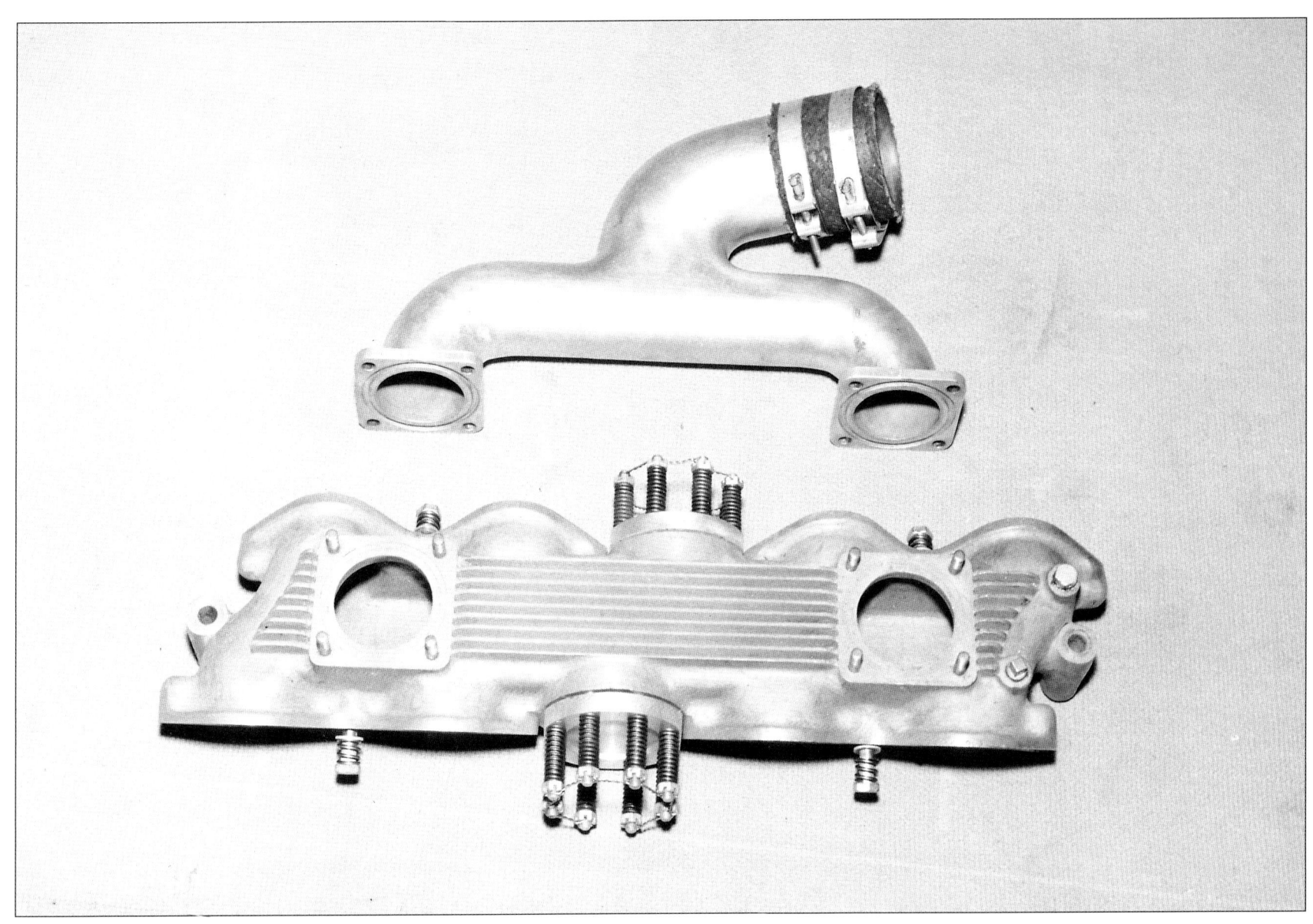

For the 1953 Indianapolis 500 Lew Welch and Jean Marcenac decided to eliminate the heavy intercooler atop the engine. Taking the place of its complicated manifolding was a new inlet manifold equipped with two spring-loaded valves to vent pressure to the atmosphere in case of a backfire. The aluminum manifold was fed by a Y-pipe.

Without the intercooler, delivery of the fresh charge from the supercharger came directly to the central manifold instead of being piped through the hole in one of the cylinder blocks. To counter the failures experienced the previous year, the long shaft driving the supercharger was strengthened. One Novi crashed in practice in 1953, killing Chet Miller in an accident closely resembling that of Ralph Hepburn, while Duke Nalon drove his Novi to 11th place after eight pit stops.

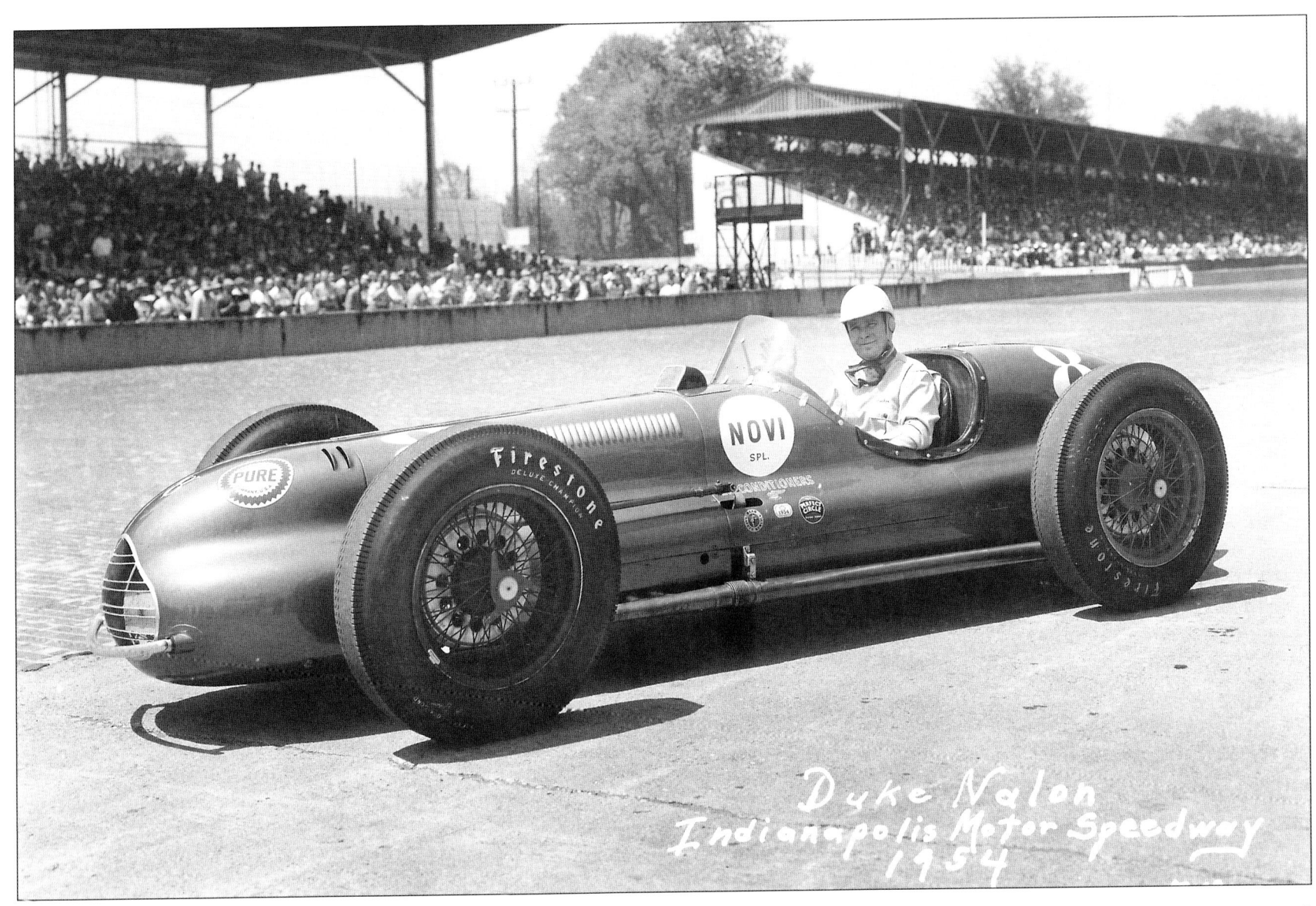

Two disappointing years for the sole remaining front-drive Novi began in 1954. A new blue paint scheme recaptured some of the glamour of the original appearance of a complete Novi racing car in 1946. With the arrival of the low Kurtis "roadsters," however, front-wheel drive was no longer the fast way around the Speedway. Duke Nalon qualified at 136.395 mph but was ignominiously bumped from the starting field by faster cars.

Equipped since 1954 with a new Bendix aircraft-type carburetor, the now-white Novi looked dramatically different in 1955 with its Halibrand magnesium wheels. Behind them were new disc brakes from the same source. 1952 Indy winner Troy Ruttman, pictured, tried the Novi after the 1954 race and was Lew Welch's choice to qualify it in 1955. Their effort was halted by the breakage of transaxle parts for which no spares were available.

Shown without its supercharger on the dynamometer of Jean Marcenac's workshop in California, the Novi V-8 reverted to a Holley aircraft carburetor in 1956, mounted horizontally to suit a new rear-drive chassis. Its maximum output at that time was 650 bhp at 7,500 rpm.

For the 1956 Indy 500 Lew Welch took the dramatic step of commissioning new rear-drive chassis from Frank Kurtis for his two Novi V-8s. As was Indy practice at the time the new 500F chassis had solid axles at both front and rear and was sprung by torsion bars. The frame was tubular steel.

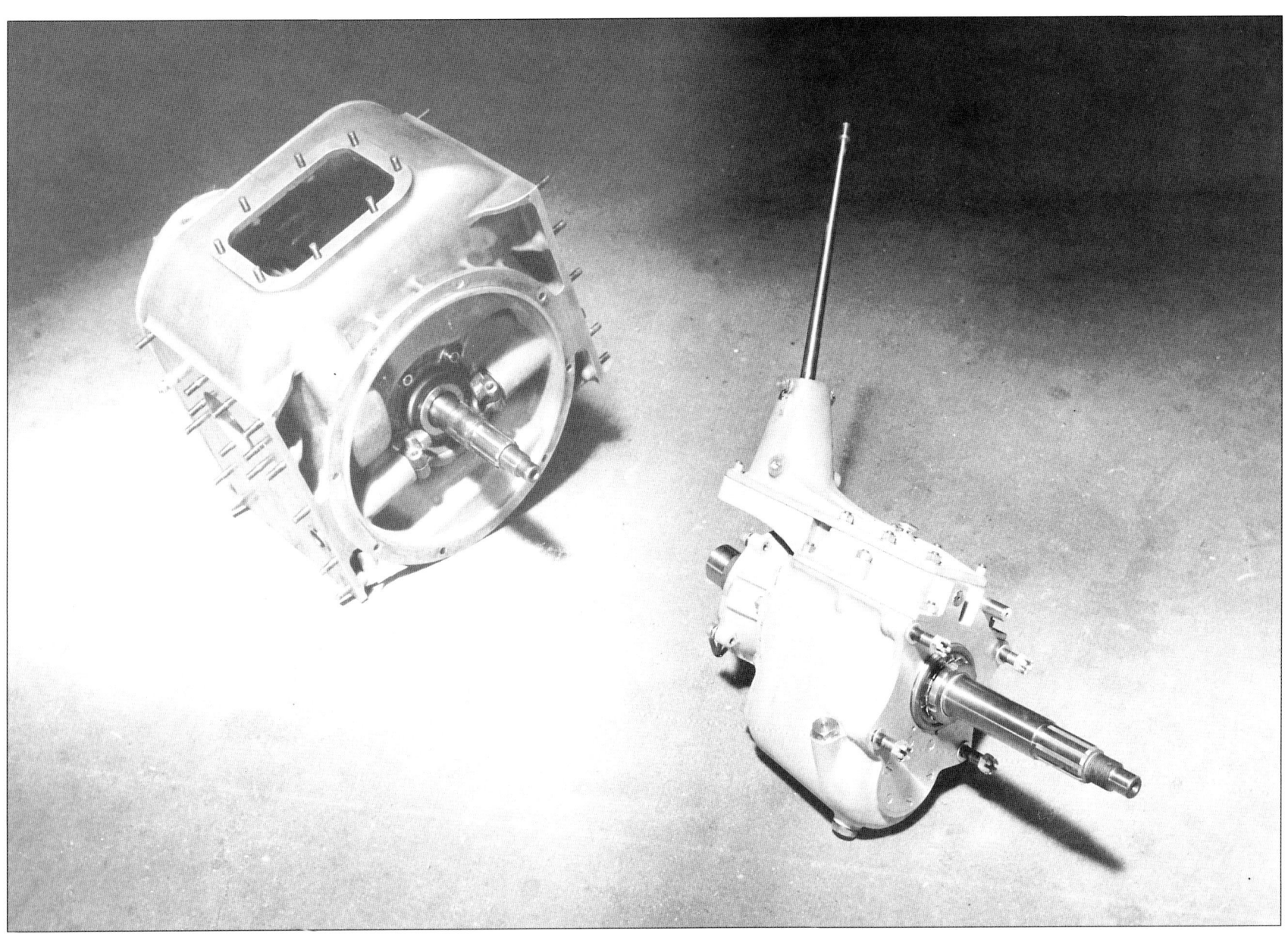

On the left is the transaxle of the original front-drive Novi while on the right is the 3-speed transmission of Meyer-Drake origin used with the new 1956 rear-drive car. The Novi engines required new crankcase castings to suit the new transmission's different mounting arrangement.

In the cockpit of the new 1956 Novi the shift lever was high on the left. Fuel flow from the car's two tanks, one of which was at the driver's left, was controlled by a floor-mounted valve. Marked on the tachometer was the engine's operating range, extending up to 7,600 rpm.

To suit the Indy Speedway's left-hand turns the drive train of the 1956 Novi was offset significantly to the left side. The offset from the car's centerline was four inches to the left and the engine sat two inches lower in the chassis than it had previously.

A bird's-eye view of the engine room of the 1956 Novi showed the Holley carburetor feeding the front-mounted supercharger. To race at Monza in 1957, as shown, the Novi carried both tubular and rotary shock absorbers and wore Firestone road-racing tires.

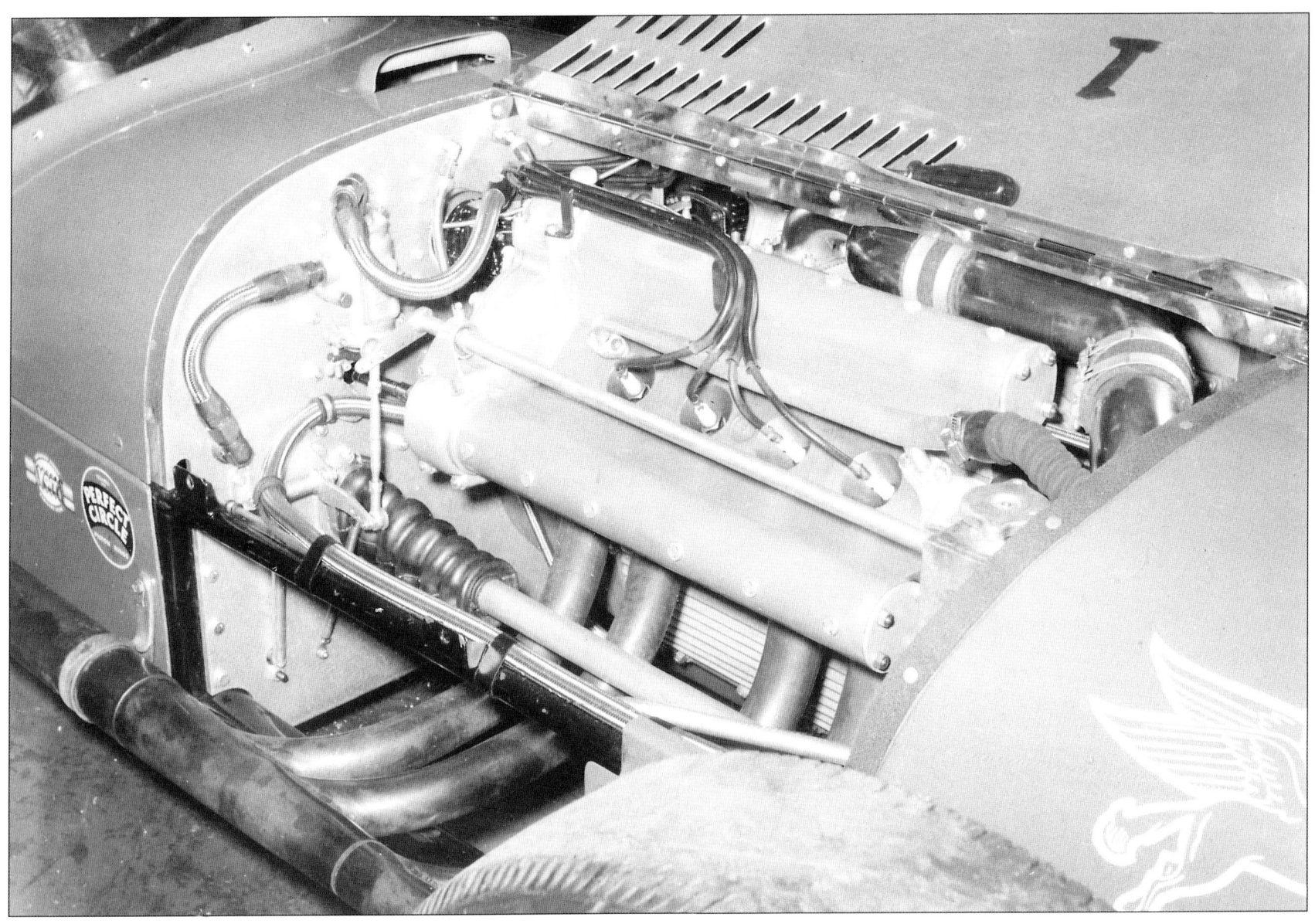

Incredibly, the new rear-drive Novis were completed by the Frank Kurtis shop in time for the 1956 500-mile race at the end of May after being commissioned in January of the same year. Superb design made the powerful V-8 look right at home in its new environment.

Passing the engine on the right side of the chassis was the drag link from the cockpit-mounted steering box. This pulled and pushed a bell crank, which in turn controlled the tie rods that steered the front wheel. This replaced the two drag links that had been used in the front-drive chassis. Watt linkages guided the front and rear solid axles.

A novelty on the 1956 rear-drive Novi was the use of a vacuum booster to assist braking. Paul Russo experienced braking problems with this car during practice. His brother Eddie was waiting in line with Novi number 31 to qualify but time ran out before he had an opportunity to try to make the race.

In his garage in the Speedway's Gasoline Alley, Jean Marcenac discussed the progress of the new Novis with Speedway owner Anton "Tony" Hulman. The two Speedway veterans were great friends. Marcenac was famous for working long hours on his charges, often sleeping in the garage rather than taking time to travel to his lodgings.

With a wheelbase of 96 inches, 8 inches shorter than their front-driven predecessors, the new 1956 Novi roadsters were significantly lighter. The scoop above the nose provided air to the carburetor while the scoop on the cowl cooled the magneto. A cylindrical aircraft-type oil cooler protruded from the left side of the body.

Although no longer active as a driver, Duke Nalon was still employed by Lew Welch in his network of auto equipment stores. With those stores newly carrying Italian Vespa motor scooters, Nalon posed on one at Indy in 1956 next to Paul Russo's Vespa Special Novi. No greater contrast in motorized equipment is imaginable.

While Paul Russo was firmly settled in the seat of Novi number 29 in 1956, Duke Nalon—here walking beside Paul—turned some laps in the sister car as a favor to Welch. The team owner greatly valued Nalon's long experience with the powerful Novi.

Lew Welch, on right, and Jean Marcenac confer with Paul Russo, an Indy veteran who had first tried a front-drive Novi in 1955. Behind Welch and Russo, in a dark suit, was Chicagoan Andy Granatelli, a former driver who had been bewitched by the Novi since he saw Ralph Hepburn race the original car ten years earlier.

When they first appeared at the Speedway in 1956 the Novis had screens for their front air scoops. These were later removed. On a resurfaced Indy oval, Russo was instantly among the fastest contenders in 1956, lapping at 146.6 mph. The Novis were immediately made favorites for pole position.

In the event Russo's qualifying time was a disappointing 143.546 mph, placing him eighth in the starting field. By the 11th lap of the race Russo moved into what appeared to be an easy lead, lapping at better than 144 mph. On lap 21, however, a burst tire knocked his Novi into the wall and out of the race.

Architects of the new Novi era at Indy were Jean Marcenac, right, and Frank Kurtis. They had married an engine that represented the best in traditional Indy racing technology to a chassis that incorporated everything Kurtis had learned about how to go quickly around Indy's 2½-mile four-cornered oval. The new rear-drive car seemed to have everything needed to win the rich 500-mile race.

In 1957 Paul Russo's Novi wore car number 54, a particular favorite of Lew Welch. It retained the distinctive finned headrest that enhanced the already aggressive look of the rear-drive Novis. The contours of his Firestone tires are already "feathered" from some high-speed lapping.

New Indy rules for 1957 limited the size of supercharged engines to 171 cubic inches or 2.8 liters. To meet this requirement the V-8's bore remained at 3.19 inches but the stroke was reduced to 2.625 inches (66.7 mm). Other changes included the restoration of front grilles and removal of the external oil cooler on the left side of the car. Paul Russo posed with his car next to Tony Bettenhausen in its sister.

Paul Russo could justifiably be pleased with his qualifying time for the 1957 500: quickest of all entries at 144.817 mph including a fastest lap of 145.255 mph. In the light-blue sister car, Bettenhausen's qualifying speed was 142.439 mph. Both Novis were in the 1957 Indy 500.

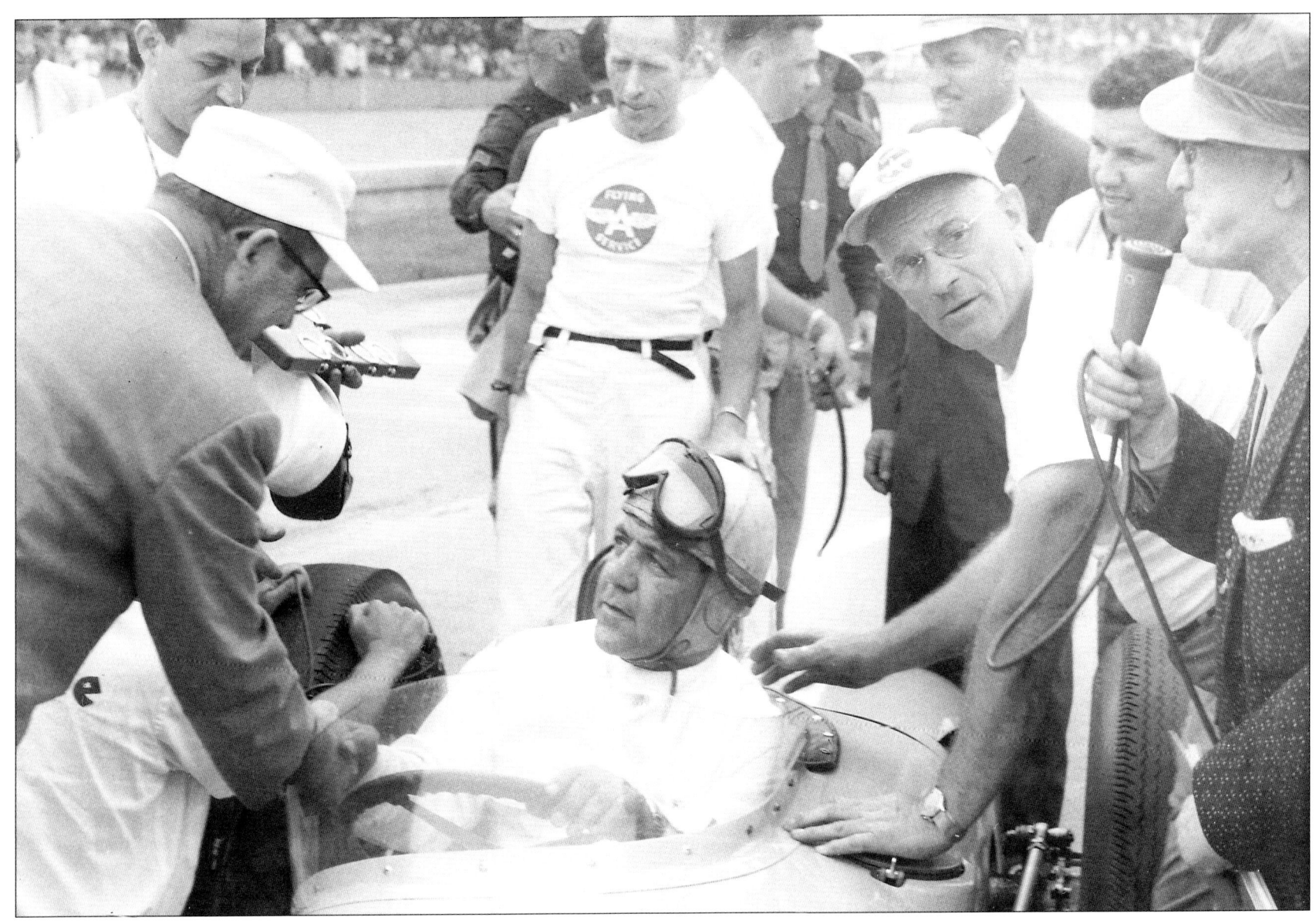

Lew Welch showed with a hearty handshake how pleased he was with Russo's excellent qualifying effort in 1957. Mechanic Radio Gardner was at right while a track announcer prepared to interview Russo. Seasoned as they were after their first year in 1956, the new rear-drive Novis should have been strong contenders to win but had to be satisfied with a best finishing position of fourth.

Starting from 10th position, Paul Russo's Novi took the lead in 1957 on lap 12. He was still leading after 75 miles, setting a record for that distance of 140.002 mph. However, he could not match the pace of the new Offy-powered Belond Special of Sam Hanks, here running third. When Hanks passed Russo on lap 36 the Novi had no answer.

Although Paul Russo chased Sam Hanks hard in the 1957 Indy 500, the low-built Hanks car had a crucial advantage in the turns. The sister Novi of Bettenhausen started 22nd in 1957, but moved to third behind Russo and Hanks after 30 laps. However, problems with his throttle linkage left Bettenhausen five laps behind and in 15th place at the finish.

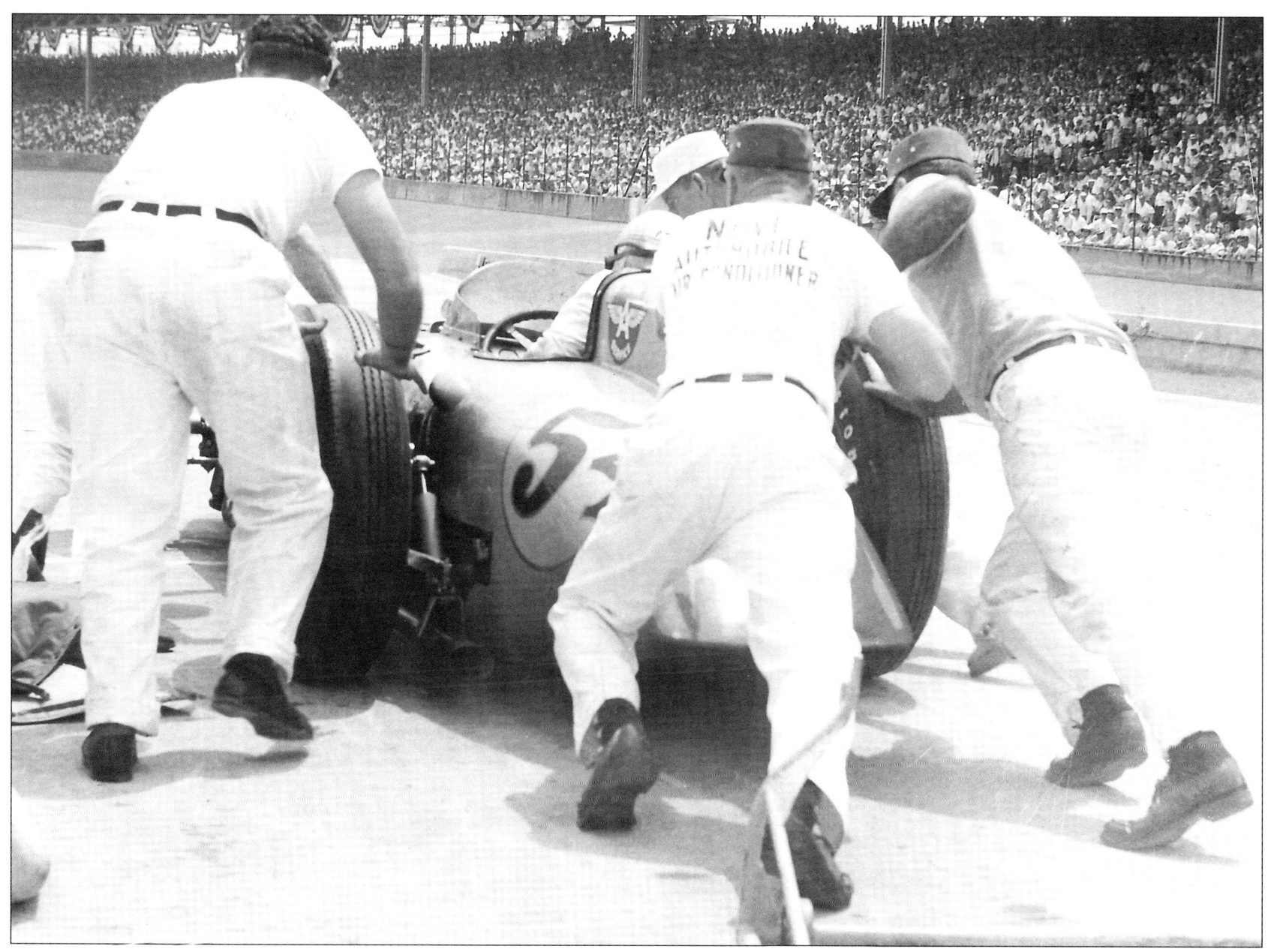

After 90 laps of the 1957 500 Paul Russo pitted for fuel and fresh tires. He placed fourth in the race, this being the first time since 1948 that a Novi had been running healthily throughout the 200 laps.

The Novi's under-hood hardware was invariably impressive. A substantial radiator was needed to cope with the cooling requirements of its engine, by far the most powerful in use at the Indianapolis Motor Speedway. Except for their trips to Monza in 1957 and to Atlanta in 1965 the Novis raced only once a year in the 500-mile event.

A major change for 1958 was the building of new cylinder blocks to allow the fitting of dual ignition. The two plugs per cylinder were fired by a special German Bosch magneto that had been developed in 1954 for use on the Formula 1 Mercedes-Benz. The twin plugs were placed vertically and as close together as possible in each cylinder.

External changes to the Novis for 1958 included a reshaped nose cone and grille and a larger cooling scoop for the new Bosch magneto. Painted a metallic blue-gray, Paul Russo's car bore number 15 in recognition of his 15th-place finish in the previous year's driver championship.

A striking feature of the revised Novis of 1958 was the more prominent fin behind the driver's headrest. A hatted Lew Welch was behind the car and Jean Marcenac was at its nose. Driver Paul Russo was at right.

In 1958 it was the Novi's turn to bump another car from the field when Bill Cheesbourg qualified car 54 at 142.546 mph. This followed a hectic repair session on the final Sunday of qualifying to replace a broken cam-drive gear. In only his second year at the Speedway, Cheesbourg was piloting one of the powerful Novis, and mighty well.

Paul Russo qualified car 15 in 14th position for the 1958 race at 142.959 mph. Modified for 1958, the Novis now had the drag link from the steering gear mounted externally. It steered the right front wheel, from which a track rod extended across to the left front wheel.

High temperatures at the Speedway in 1958 held no terrors for Cheesbourg, who hailed from Phoenix, Arizona. He took to the infield from his 33rd starting position to avoid a first-lap crash and in spite of the tweaked front axle that resulted Cheesbourg was able to bring his Novi home in tenth place.

Side by side in 1958 the two Novis made a handsome sight, Cheesbourg ahead of Russo. The Novis still had the power to pass ordinary cars on the straights but with more weight than their rivals and a heavy fuel load they were at a disadvantage in the turns.

In the cockpit of Novi number 54, Bill Cheesbourg said that he lost 15 pounds during the running of the 1958 Indy 500. His chase of Al Keller in a Kurtis-Offy ended with Cheesbourg 10th and Keller 11th.

The new low-profile Offy-powered cars like the one driven by George Amick in the 1958 race were capable of higher speeds through the turns that nullified the power advantage of the Novi. Paul Russo's pursuing number 15 Novi suffered nose-cone damage in that year's first-lap crash. Between radiator damage and a faulty throttle linkage—a chronic Novi problem—Russo had to call it quits after 122 of the 200 laps.

The Novis failed to qualify at Indy in 1959, 1960, 1961 and 1962, in the latter two years under the stewardship of new owners, the Granatelli brothers, who acquired the cars in April 1961 from Lew Welch for a reported $10,000. In 1963 Joe Granatelli changed the spark plugs of a Novi engine he and his brothers had extensively modified.

Still in the STP-sponsored Granatelli stable in 1963 was one of the 1956 chassis, fitted with a high tail fin. A teardrop-shaped oil tank was mounted on the left exterior of the body. Indy rookie Art Malone qualified the old car at 148.343 mph, an outstanding result. Gearbox and engine problems ended his race after 18 laps.

Taking advantage of a much more comprehensive dynamometer test facility than had been available to Jean Marcenac in the Lew Welch days, the Granatellis developed the Novi engines at Paxton Products in Santa Monica, California. In addition to diagnosing the doubling of the ignition advance, as described by Andy Granatelli in his introduction, the brothers and their engineers made extensive changes to the engine. To obtain improved mid-range power, new cylinder blocks were made with smaller valves and ports to induce higher gas speeds. The new blocks were stiffened by additional webbing at the ends and by smaller access ports in the water jackets.

A fine cutaway drawing of the Novi V-8 by Clarence La Tourette showed its 1963 configuration as modified by the Granatellis. The cam followers now had radiused instead of flat tops and were keyed to their guides to prevent rotation. New forged pistons provided a compression ratio of 8:1. Visible at the front are the gears driving the centrifugal supercharger and the bevel gears by means of which an external starter motor was engaged from the side—a relic of the old front-drive installation.

A maker of superchargers, the Granatellis' Paxton Company carried out development of this crucial component of the Novi engine. An impeller is seen here on a balancing bench next to a selection of the inducer vanes that were used at the point of air entry. On the table were some of the step-up drive gears used with the blower.

A supercharger impeller with its drive gear was among Novi V-8 parts set out for inspection. Adjacent to it were a forged-steel connecting rod and two forged aluminum full-skirt pistons. Retention of the piston pin was changed by the Granatellis from aluminum buttons to circlips.

Circular units at the left rear of the Novi engine as it was being prepared for racing in 1964 were the two elements of the Bosch dual magneto that triggered the engine's twin ignition. The hole through the middle of each cylinder block was now used to carry a crankcase breather up to the center of the engine's vee, there being no room to accommodate the breathers outside the camshaft housings.

As revised for 1964 the Novi engine had four water offtakes from each cylinder head instead of the original two. Lighter parts throughout the engine reduced its weight to 470 pounds. Induction was now through a Bendix injection-type carburetor, adapted by Paxton and mounted remotely from the front of the supercharger.

For the 1962 Indy 500 the Granatellis commissioned two new 500K chassis from Frank Kurtis. The new cars had their engines set 7 inches more to the rear and more sharply to the left to improve traction and reduce tire wear. Dry weight was reduced to 1,740 pounds. Indy rookie Bobby Unser qualified 500K-Novi number 6 at 149.421 mph but crashed out of the race on his second lap.

In 1963 Art Malone in his older Novi was in the foreground and behind him Jim "Hercules" Hurtubise, who qualified in the middle of the front row at a spectacular 150.257 mph. Hurtubise led the first lap and was among the top contenders when, at mid-race, he was forced by the stewards to retire with an apparent oil leak.

A new era in Novi history began in August 1963 when Andy Granatelli invited Britain's Ferguson Research Limited to bring its P99 four-wheel-drive car of only 2½ unblown liters to the Indy Speedway for tests. Although having only 220 bhp, the P99 lapped at 142 mph in the hands of Indy regular Bobby Marshman. It achieved excellent speeds in the turns—just what the Novi needed.

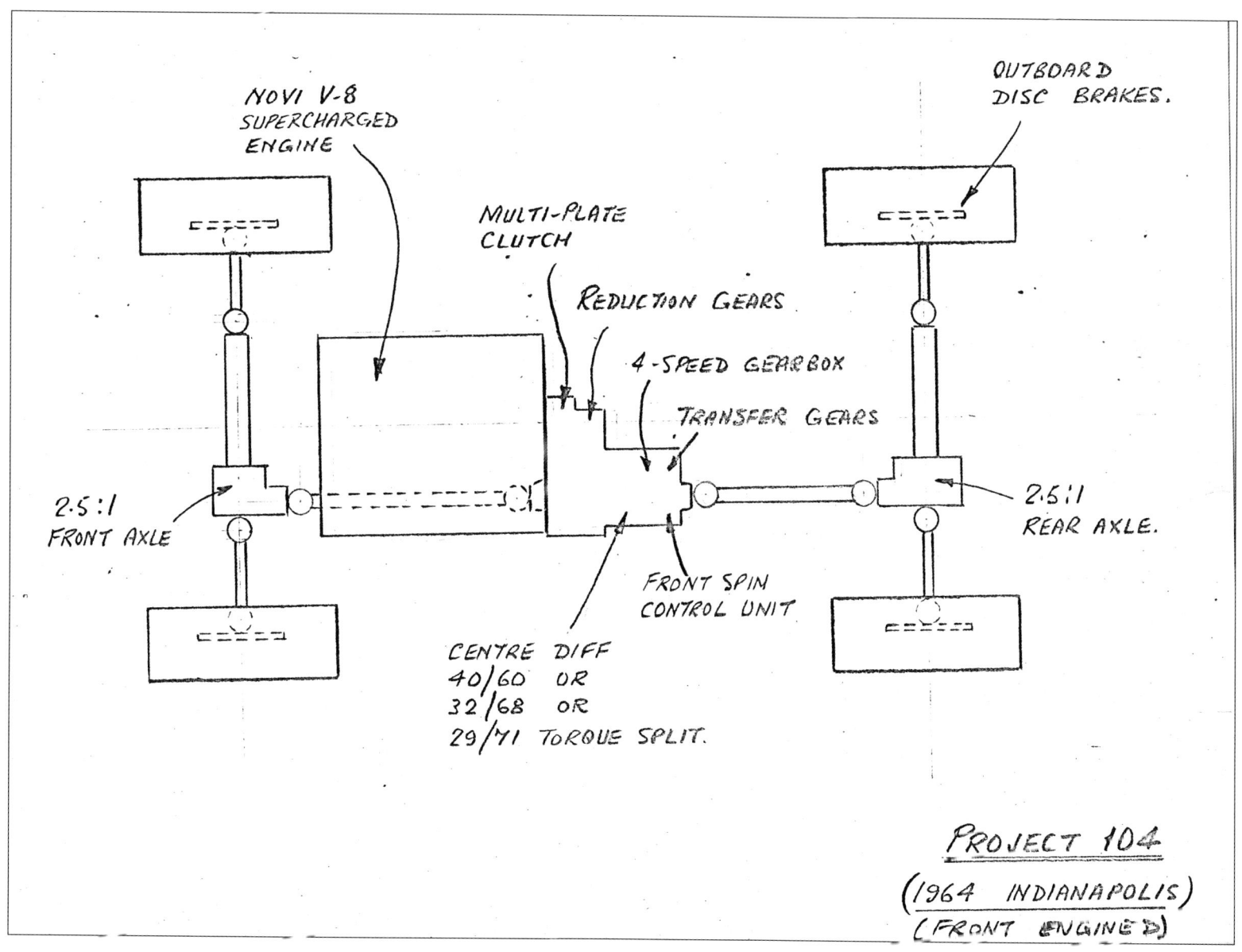

Andy Granatelli commissioned Ferguson to design and build a four-wheel-drive chassis for his Novi engine. Ferguson produced this as its Project 104, for which it had to create not only the drive line but also the complete chassis and suspension. Work on the car began at Ferguson in Coventry, England, on November 25, 1963, following completion of a preliminary study funded by Granatelli in September.

Around a spare engine provided by Paxton, the Ferguson engineers designed and constructed a mock-up of their planned racing car. This allowed checks to be made of any possible interference between the components and also served to evaluate the driving position.

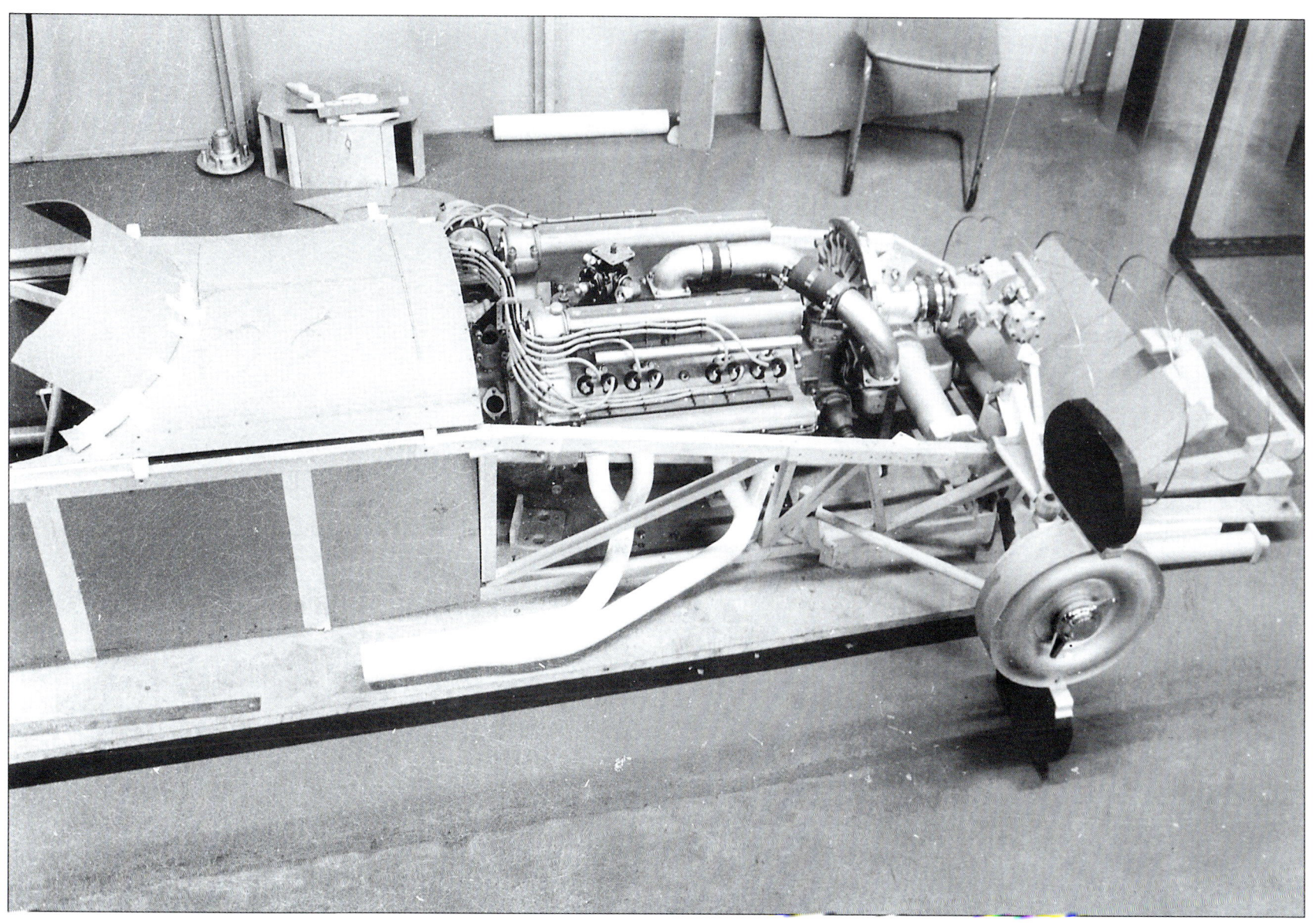

As in previous front-engined Novis, the Ferguson P104 offset the engine and drive line to the left side of the car to produce the weight distribution most advantageous for the Indy 500. The mock-up showed wheels of only 13 inches in diameter, which like the tires were specially made by Dunlop to suit the car. Four-wheel drive allowed the use of smaller wheels and tires of identical size at all four corners.

An important objective of the P104 project was weight control, in view of the added weight of the four-wheel-drive system. A multi-tubular steel space frame was designed around the engine and drive components by the Ferguson engineers. The complex transmission rested on an adjoining workbench. In the event, however, the Granatellis would be disappointed to find the car heavier than they had been given to expect.

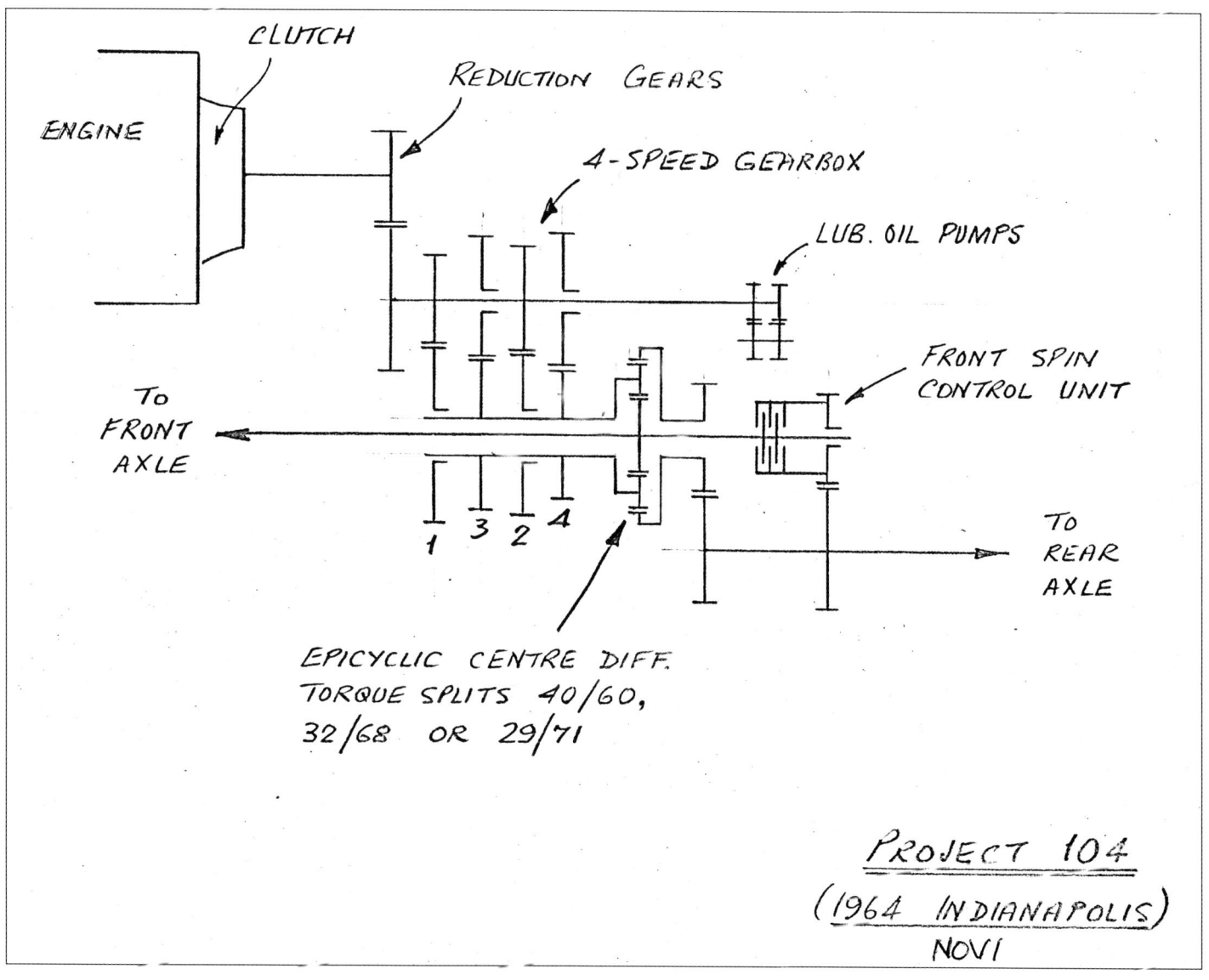

Ferguson had developed unique and proprietary concepts for the efficient use of four-wheel drive, especially in racing cars. They designed and built a special gearbox for the P104-Novi chassis that had reduction gears at the entry to the transmission, which had four speeds forward. Alternative center differentials allowed different allocations of torque, as shown, between the front and rear pairs of wheels.

The choice of square tubes throughout the P104 chassis was a practical measure that permitted ready attachment of the necessary fittings and brackets. The use of rack-and-pinion steering represented a radical advance on the systems previously used in Novi chassis. Below the scroll of the supercharger was the drive to the right side of the chassis used to start the engine.

In combining the famed Novi V-8 with an advanced four-wheel-drive chassis, the new car represented one of the most complex racing machines ever attempted. The use of four-wheel drive had originally been suggested to Andy Granatelli by Stirling Moss, who had successfully competed in the Ferguson P99 at Britain's Oulton Park.

To the left of the driver's feet in the P104-Novi was the transfer case taking the drive to the four-speed gearbox. This then powered the drive shafts to the front and rear differentials. The seldom-used clutch pedal was suspended while the brake pedal pivoted from floor level. The engine's siamesed magneto is visible at the left.

The Novi-Ferguson's frame strength was enhanced by the addition of aluminum sheets to the side members, giving a semi-stressed characteristic to the crucial central cockpit area. Fuel tanks were fitted within the compartments at the sides and in the tail as well, adding up to a total capacity of 74½ gallons.

Independent rear suspension was a novelty for a Novi. It was achieved by means of parallel wishbones, the upper member having an adjustable link for control of toe-in. The upper wishbone extended inboard to actuate a concentric coil-shock unit. Dunlop provided the 11-inch disc brakes.

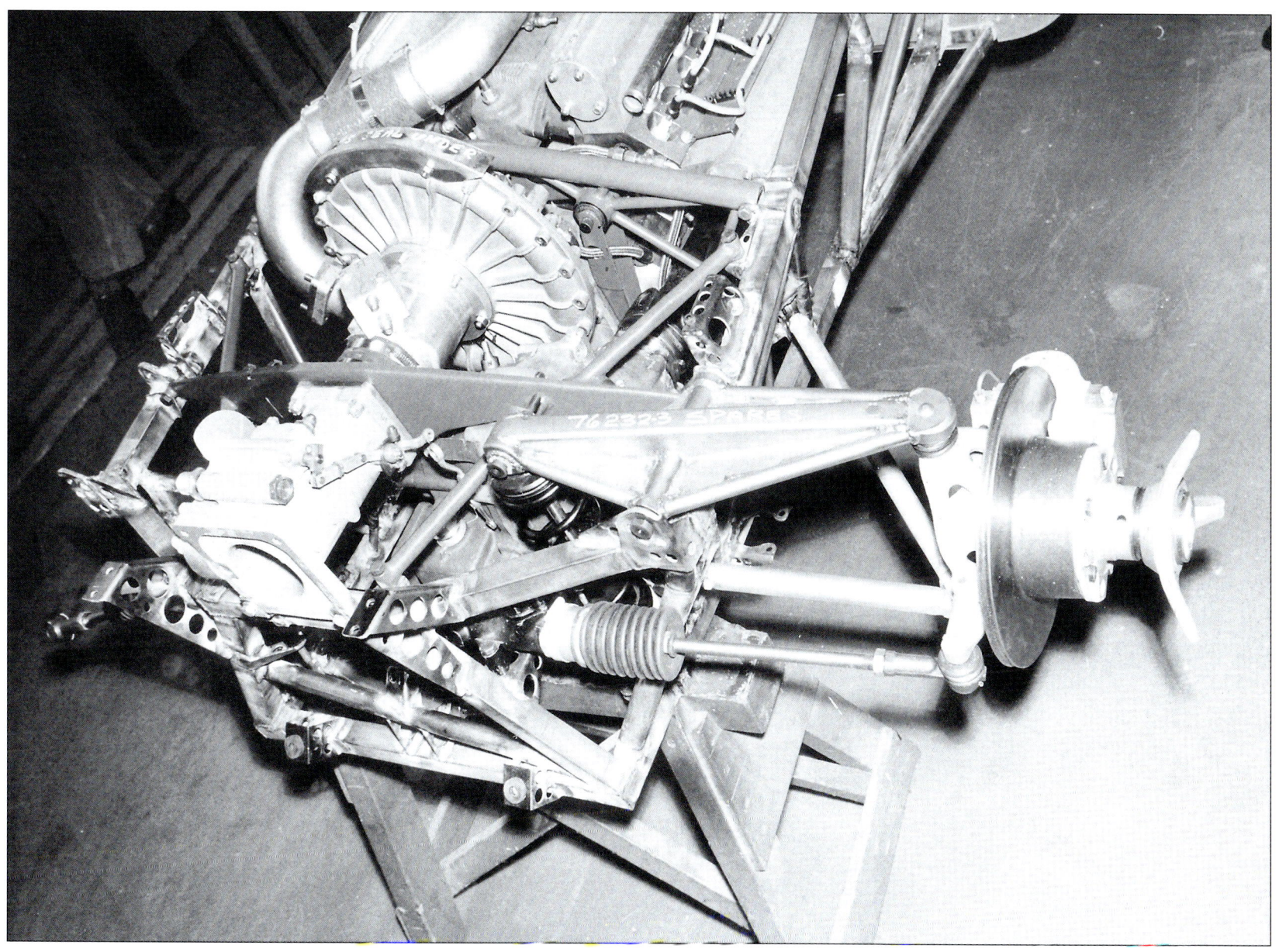

At the front of the 1964 Novi-Ferguson the upper suspension arms extended inboard to operate coil-shock units, clearing space outboard for the drive shafts to the front wheels. The shafts were not in position here. The rack-and-pinion steering gear was placed forward of the front wheels.

Remarkably the new Studebaker STP Special—as it was named—was ready for testing at the Speedway on March 28, 1964. Andy Granatelli was at the wheel for some of the first laps taken by the new car, which was then unpainted. Bobby Unser, given the assignment in May to attempt to qualify the radical racer, was being briefed here by Andy.

A purposeful-looking racing car by any standards, the Novi-Ferguson was fitted with a protective rear "nerf bar." A single fuel filler at the rear delivered methanol to all three of its main tanks. The chassis alone represented an investment of $175,000 by Paxton and STP and a Novi engine was valued at $55,000.

At the front of the Novi-Ferguson an anti-roll bar, linked to the front suspension, passed through the chamber that admitted air to the Bendix injection-type carburetor. A new supercharger housing carried the name of the Granatellis' company, Paxton Products.

The right side of the engine bay of the 1964 Novi-Ferguson well illustrated the integration of engine and chassis achieved by the Ferguson designers under Claude Hill. A suitable chassis had been created for the most powerful racing engine then in existence, producing 742 bhp at 8,200 rpm. It was capable of speeds up to 9,000 rpm.

For their first attempt under heavy time pressure the Ferguson engineers succeeded in giving the Studebaker STP Special a certain sense of style. It rested on a wheelbase of 100 inches with front and rear track dimensions of 60 inches and weighed in at some 2,400 pounds, 400 pounds more than its designers and purchasers had hoped.

Oiling problems experienced with the Novi-Ferguson in its early testing were solved by installing a special tank on the left side of the chassis. Although the car was tested on other tires, including Goodyears and Firestones, it raced on Dunlop tires. Bobby Unser qualified it at 154.865 mph, fifth fastest in 1964, but was knocked out of the race by a multiple crash on the second lap.

At the 1965 500-mile race Andy Granatelli talked with brother Vince, who was sporting the STP garb that set the crew apart. The Granatellis built a lighter four-wheel-drive Novi for the 1965 race but this crashed badly on the day before qualifying commenced and was not able to compete.

Andy Granatelli pitched in to assist in preparing the Novi-Ferguson for 1965 duty after the newer car crashed. The Ferguson chassis was now running on Firestone tires.

Stepping into the older four-wheel-drive Novi in 1965 after the newer car crashed, Bobby Unser put it in the field with a four-lap average of 157.567 mph—the fastest a Novi would ever qualify at Indy. He was eighth fastest and the only front-engined car in the field.

As a mark of distinction the Novi-Ferguson was given white-wall tires for the race. Bobby Unser kept the big red car in the top 10 until it was stopped on lap 69 by a failure of a fitting in the oil line to the supercharger. Thereafter no Novi would turn a wheel in a 500-mile race at Indianapolis.

One of the rear-drive Novis built in 1962 was still racing in 1965, although the main emphasis was on the new four-wheel-drive cars. The Kurtis-built car was qualified by Jim Hurtubise at 156.863 mph, tenth fastest in the field. The Novi, featured on our cover, was out after the first lap with a failed transmission.

The sight of STP crew members pushing car 59 to one side in 1965 serves as an evocative symbol of the end of the active racing career of the immortal Novis. Later that year the car finished fourth at Atlanta in a 250-mile race, the first and only time since Monza in 1957 that the Novis competed at a track other than Indianapolis.

After its retirement from competition following the 1963 race, one of the 500F-chassis Novis remained at the STP Corporation offices at Des Plaines, Illinois. A glossy paint scheme suited it for display at auto shows and in the promotional activities of the Granatellis and STP.

The veteran Novi-Kurtis, dating from 1956, was a glamorous backdrop when Andy Granatelli posed in 1969 with a snowmobile he was planning to use on a lake near his Chicago home. The long and remarkable saga of the Novis was now definitively at its end.

MORE TITLES FROM ICONOGRAFIX:

AMERICAN CULTURE
AMERICAN SERVICE STATIONS 1935-1943 PHOTO ARCHIVE	ISBN 1-882256-27-1
COCA-COLA: A HISTORY IN PHOTOGRAPHS 1930-1969	ISBN 1-882256-46-8
COCA-COLA: ITS VEHICLES IN PHOTOGRAPHS 1930-1969	ISBN 1-882256-47-6
PHILLIPS 66 1945-1954 PHOTO ARCHIVE	ISBN 1-882256-42-5

AUTOMOTIVE
CADILLAC 1948-1964 PHOTO ALBUM	ISBN 1-882256-83-2
CAMARO 1967-2000 PHOTO ARCHIVE	ISBN 1-58388-032-1
CORVETTE THE EXOTIC EXPERIMENTAL CARS, LUDVIGSEN LIBRARY SERIES	ISBN 1-58388-017-8
CORVETTE PROTOTYPES & SHOW CARS PHOTO ALBUM	ISBN 1-882256-77-8
EARLY FORD V-8S 1932-1942 PHOTO ALBUM	ISBN 1-882256-97-2
IMPERIAL 1955-1963 PHOTO ARCHIVE	ISBN 1-882256-22-0
IMPERIAL 1964-1968 PHOTO ARCHIVE	ISBN 1-882256-23-9
LINCOLN MOTOR CARS 1920-1942 PHOTO ARCHIVE	ISBN 1-882256-57-3
LINCOLN MOTOR CARS 1946-1960 PHOTO ARCHIVE	ISBN 1-882256-58-1
PACKARD MOTOR CARS 1935-1942 PHOTO ARCHIVE	ISBN 1-882256-44-1
PACKARD MOTOR CARS 1946-1958 PHOTO ARCHIVE	ISBN 1-882256-45-X
PONTIAC DREAM CARS, SHOW CARS & PROTOTYPES 1928-1998 PHOTO ALBUM	ISBN 1-882256-93-X
PONTIAC FIREBIRD TRANS-AM 1969-1999 PHOTO ALBUM	ISBN 1-882256-95-6
PONTIAC FIREBIRD 1967-2000 PHOTO HISTORY	ISBN 1-58388-028-3
STUDEBAKER 1933-1942 PHOTO ARCHIVE	ISBN 1-882256-24-7
ULTIMATE CORVETTE TRIVIA CHALLENGE	ISBN 1-58388-035-6

BUSES
BUSES OF MOTOR COACH INDUSTRIES 1932-2000 PHOTO ARCHIVE	ISBN 1-58388-039-9
THE GENERAL MOTORS NEW LOOK BUS PHOTO ARCHIVE	ISBN 1-58388-007-0
GREYHOUND BUSES 1914-2000 PHOTO ARCHIVE	ISBN 1-58388-027-5
MACK® BUSES 1900-1960 PHOTO ARCHIVE*	ISBN 1-58388-020-8
TRAILWAYS BUSES 1936-2001 PHOTO ARCHIVE	ISBN 1-58388-029-1

EMERGENCY VEHICLES
AMERICAN LAFRANCE 700 SERIES 1945-1952 PHOTO ARCHIVE	ISBN 1-882256-90-5
AMERICAN LAFRANCE 700 SERIES 1945-1952 PHOTO ARCHIVE VOLUME 2	ISBN 1-58388-025-9
AMERICAN LAFRANCE 700 & 800 SERIES 1953-1958 PHOTO ARCHIVE	ISBN 1-882256-91-3
AMERICAN LAFRANCE 900 SERIES 1958-1964 PHOTO ARCHIVE	ISBN 1-58388-002-X
CLASSIC AMERICAN AMBULANCES 1900-1979 PHOTO ARCHIVE	ISBN 1-882256-94-8
CLASSIC AMERICAN FUNERAL VEHICLES 1900-1980 PHOTO ARCHIVE	ISBN 1-58388-016-X
CLASSIC AMERICAN LIMOUSINES 1955-2000 PHOTO ARCHIVE	ISBN 1-58388-041-0
CLASSIC SEAGRAVE 1935-1951 PHOTO ARCHIVE	ISBN 1-58388-034-8
FIRE CHIEF CARS 1900-1997 PHOTO ALBUM	ISBN 1-882256-87-5
LOS ANGELES CITY FIRE APPARATUS 1953 - 1999 PHOTO ARCHIVE	ISBN 1-58388-012-7
MACK MODEL C FIRE TRUCKS 1957-1967 PHOTO ARCHIVE*	ISBN 1-58388-014-3
MACK MODEL CF FIRE TRUCKS 1967-1981 PHOTO ARCHIVE*	ISBN 1-882256-63-8
MACK MODEL L FIRE TRUCKS 1940-1954 PHOTO ARCHIVE*	ISBN 1-882256-86-7
NAVY & MARINE CORPS FIRE APPARATUS 1836 -2000 PHOTO GALLERY	ISBN 1-58388-031-3
PIERCE ARROW FIRE APPARATUS 1979-1998 PHOTO ARCHIVE	ISBN 1-58388-023-2
POLICE CARS: RESTORING, COLLECTING & SHOWING AMERICA'S FINEST SEDANS	ISBN 1-58388-046-1
SEAGRAVE 70TH ANNIVERSARY SERIES PHOTO ARCHIVE	ISBN 1-58388-001-1
VOLUNTEER & RURAL FIRE APPARATUS PHOTO GALLERY	ISBN 1-58388-005-4
WARD LAFRANCE FIRE TRUCKS 1918-1978 PHOTO ARCHIVE	ISBN 1-58388-013-5
YOUNG FIRE EQUIPMENT 1932-1991 PHOTO ARCHIVE	ISBN 1-58388-015-1

RACING
GT40 PHOTO ARCHIVE	ISBN 1-882256-64-6
INDY CARS OF THE 1950s, LUDVIGSEN LIBRARY SERIES	ISBN 1-58388-018-6
INDIANAPOLIS RACING CARS OF FRANK KURTIS 1941-1963 PHOTO ARCHIVE	ISBN 1-58388-026-7
JUAN MANUEL FANGIO WORLD CHAMPION DRIVER SERIES PHOTO ALBUM	ISBN 1-58388-008-9
LE MANS 1950: THE BRIGGS CUNNINGHAM CAMPAIGN PHOTO ARCHIVE	ISBN 1-882256-21-2
MARIO ANDRETTI WORLD CHAMPION DRIVER SERIES PHOTO ALBUM	ISBN 1-58388-009-7
NOVI V-8 INDY CARS 1941-1965 KARL LUDVIGSEN LIBRARY SERIES	ISBN 1-58388-037-2
SEBRING 12-HOUR RACE 1970 PHOTO ARCHIVE	ISBN 1-882256-20-4
VANDERBILT CUP RACE 1936 & 1937 PHOTO ARCHIVE	ISBN 1-882256-66-2

RAILWAYS
CHICAGO, ST. PAUL, MINNEAPOLIS & OMAHA RAILWAY 1880-1940 PHOTO ARCHIVE	ISBN 1-882256-67-0
CHICAGO & NORTH WESTERN RAILWAY 1975-1995 PHOTO ARCHIVE	ISBN 1-882256-76-X
GREAT NORTHERN RAILWAY 1945-1970 PHOTO ARCHIVE	ISBN 1-882256-56-5
GREAT NORTHERN RAILWAY 1945-1970 VOL 2 PHOTO ARCHIVE	ISBN 1-882256-79-4
MILWAUKEE ROAD 1850-1960 PHOTO ARCHIVE	ISBN 1-882256-61-1
MILWAUKEE ROAD DEPOTS 1856-1954 PHOTO ARCHIVE	ISBN 1-58388-040-2
SHOW TRAINS OF THE 20TH CENTURY	ISBN 1-58388-030-5
SOO LINE 1975-1992 PHOTO ARCHIVE	ISBN 1-882256-68-9
TRAINS OF THE TWIN PORTS, DULUTH-SUPERIOR IN THE 1950s PHOTO ARCHIVE	ISBN 1-58388-003-8
TRAINS OF THE CIRCUS 1872-1956 PHOTO ARCHIVE	ISBN 1-58388-024-0
TRAINS OF THE UPPER MIDWEST: STEAM & DIESEL IN THE 1950S & 1960S	ISBN 1-58388-036-4
WISCONSIN CENTRAL LIMITED 1987-1996 PHOTO ARCHIVE	ISBN 1-882256-75-1
WISCONSIN CENTRAL RAILWAY 1871-1909 PHOTO ARCHIVE	ISBN 1-882256-78-6

TRUCKS
BEVERAGE TRUCKS 1910-1975 PHOTO ARCHIVE	ISBN 1-882256-60-3
BROCKWAY TRUCKS 1948-1961 PHOTO ARCHIVE	ISBN 1-882256-55-7
CHEVROLET EL CAMINO PHOTO HISTORY INCL GMC SPRINT & CABALLERO	ISBN 1-58388-044-5
DODGE PICKUPS 1939-1978 PHOTO ALBUM	ISBN 1-882256-82-4
DODGE POWER WAGONS 1940-1980 PHOTO ARCHIVE	ISBN 1-882256-89-1
DODGE POWER WAGON PHOTO HISTORY	ISBN 1-58388-019-4
DODGE TRUCKS 1929-1947 PHOTO ARCHIVE	ISBN 1-882256-36-0
DODGE TRUCKS 1948-1960 PHOTO ARCHIVE	ISBN 1-882256-37-9
FORD HEAVY DUTY TRUCKS 1948-1998 PHOTO HISTORY	ISBN 1-58388-043-7
HEAVY RESCUE TRUCKS 1931-2000 PHOTO GALLERY	ISBN 1-58388-045-3
JEEP 1941-2000 PHOTO ARCHIVE	ISBN 1-58388-021-6
JEEP PROTOTYPES & CONCEPT VEHICLES PHOTO ARCHIVE	ISBN 1-58388-033-X
LOGGING TRUCKS 1915-1970 PHOTO ARCHIVE	ISBN 1-882256-59-X
MACK MODEL AB PHOTO ARCHIVE*	ISBN 1-882256-18-2
MACK AP SUPER-DUTY TRUCKS 1926-1938 PHOTO ARCHIVE*	ISBN 1-882256-54-9
MACK MODEL B 1953-1966 VOL 1 PHOTO ARCHIVE*	ISBN 1-882256-19-0
MACK MODEL B 1953-1966 VOL 2 PHOTO ARCHIVE*	ISBN 1-882256-34-4
MACK EB-EC-ED-EE-EF-EG-DE 1936-1951 PHOTO ARCHIVE*	ISBN 1-882256-29-8
MACK EH-EJ-EM-EQ-ER-ES 1936-1950 PHOTO ARCHIVE*	ISBN 1-882256-39-5
MACK FC-FCSW-NW 1936-1947 PHOTO ARCHIVE*	ISBN 1-882256-28-X
MACK FG-FH-FJ-FK-FN-FP-FT-FW 1937-1950 PHOTO ARCHIVE*	ISBN 1-882256-35-2
MACK LF-LH-LJ-LM-LT 1940-1956 PHOTO ARCHIVE*	ISBN 1-882256-38-7
MACK TRUCKS PHOTO GALLERY	ISBN 1-882256-88-3
NEW CAR CARRIERS 1910-1998 PHOTO ALBUM	ISBN 1-882256-98-0
PLYMOUTH COMMERCIAL VEHICLES PHOTO ARCHIVE	ISBN 1-58388-004-6
REFUSE & RECYCLING TRUCKS PHOTO ARCHIVE	ISBN 1-58388-042-9
STUDEBAKER TRUCKS 1927-1940 PHOTO ARCHIVE	ISBN 1-882256-40-9
STUDEBAKER TRUCKS 1941-1964 PHOTO ARCHIVE	ISBN 1-882256-41-7
WHITE TRUCKS 1900-1937 PHOTO ARCHIVE	ISBN 1-882256-80-8

TRACTORS & CONSTRUCTION EQUIPMENT
CASE TRACTORS 1912-1959 PHOTO ARCHIVE	ISBN 1-882256-32-8
CATERPILLAR PHOTO GALLERY	ISBN 1-882256-70-0
CATERPILLAR POCKET GUIDE THE TRACK-TYPE TRACTORS 1925-1957	ISBN 1-58388-022-4
CATERPILLAR D-2 & R-2 PHOTO ARCHIVE	ISBN 1-882256-99-9
CATERPILLAR D-8 1933-1974 INCLUDING DIESEL 75 & RD-8 PHOTO ARCHIVE	ISBN 1-882256-96-4
CATERPILLAR MILITARY TRACTORS VOLUME 1 PHOTO ARCHIVE	ISBN 1-882256-16-6
CATERPILLAR MILITARY TRACTORS VOLUME 2 PHOTO ARCHIVE	ISBN 1-882256-17-4
CATERPILLAR SIXTY PHOTO ARCHIVE	ISBN 1-882256-05-0
CATERPILLAR TEN INCLUDING 7C FIFTEEN & HIGH FIFTEEN PHOTO ARCHIVE	ISBN 1-58388-011-9
CATERPILLAR THIRTY 2ND ED. INC. BEST THIRTY, 6G THIRTY & R-4 PHOTO ARCHIVE	ISBN 1-58388-006-2
CLETRAC AND OLIVER CRAWLERS PHOTO ARCHIVE	ISBN 1-882256-43-3
CLASSIC AMERICAN STEAMROLLERS 1871-1935 PHOTO ARCHIVE	ISBN 1-58388-038-0
FARMALL CUB PHOTO ARCHIVE	ISBN 1-882256-71-9
FARMALL F- SERIES PHOTO ARCHIVE	ISBN 1-882256-02-6
FARMALL MODEL H PHOTO ARCHIVE	ISBN 1-882256-03-4
FARMALL MODEL M PHOTO ARCHIVE	ISBN 1-882256-15-8
FARMALL REGULAR PHOTO ARCHIVE	ISBN 1-882256-14-X
FARMALL SUPER SERIES PHOTO ARCHIVE	ISBN 1-882256-49-2
FORDSON 1917-1928 PHOTO ARCHIVE	ISBN 1-882256-33-6
HART-PARR PHOTO ARCHIVE	ISBN 1-882256-08-5
HOLT TRACTORS PHOTO ARCHIVE	ISBN 1-882256-10-7
INTERNATIONAL TRACTRACTOR PHOTO ARCHIVE	ISBN 1-882256-48-4
INTERNATIONAL TD CRAWLERS 1933-1962 PHOTO ARCHIVE	ISBN 1-882256-72-7
JOHN DEERE MODEL A PHOTO ARCHIVE	ISBN 1-882256-12-3
JOHN DEERE MODEL B PHOTO ARCHIVE	ISBN 1-882256-01-8
JOHN DEERE MODEL D PHOTO ARCHIVE	ISBN 1-882256-00-X
JOHN DEERE 30 SERIES PHOTO ARCHIVE	ISBN 1-882256-13-1
MINNEAPOLIS-MOLINE U-SERIES PHOTO ARCHIVE	ISBN 1-882256-07-7
OLIVER TRACTORS PHOTO ARCHIVE	ISBN 1-882256-09-3
RUSSELL GRADERS PHOTO ARCHIVE	ISBN 1-882256-11-5
TWIN CITY TRACTOR PHOTO ARCHIVE	ISBN 1-882256-06-9

*This product is sold under license from Mack Trucks, Inc. Mack is a registered Trademark of Mack Trucks, Inc. All rights reserved.

All Iconografix books are available from direct mail specialty book dealers and bookstores worldwide, or can be ordered from the publisher. For book trade and distribution information or to add your name to our mailing list and receive a **FREE CATALOG** contact:

Iconografix, PO Box 446, Hudson, Wisconsin, 54016   Telephone: (715) 381-9755, (800) 289-3504 (USA), Fax: (715) 381-9756

MORE GREAT BOOKS FROM ICONOGRAFIX

MARIO ANDRETTI WORLD CHAMPION DRIVER SERIES PHOTO ALBUM ISBN 1-58388-009-7

INDIANAPOLIS RACING CARS OF FRANK KURTIS 1941-1963 PHOTO ARCHIVE ISBN 1-58388-026-7

CORVETTE THE EXOTIC EXPERIMENTAL CARS, LUDVIGSEN LIBRARY SERIES ISBN 1-58388-017-8

SEBRING 12-HOUR RACE 1970 PHOTO ARCHIVE ISBN 1-882256-20-4

JUAN MANUEL FANGIO WORLD CHAMPION DRIVER SERIES PHOTO ALBUM ISBN 1-58388-008-9

INDY CARS OF THE 1950s, LUDVIGSEN LIBRARY SERIES ISBN 1-58388-018-6

VANDERBILT CUP RACE 1936 & 1937 PHOTO ARCHIVE ISBN 1-882256-66-2

ICONOGRAFIX, INC. P.O. BOX 446, DEPT BK, HUDSON, WI 54016
FOR A FREE CATALOG CALL:
1-800-289-3504

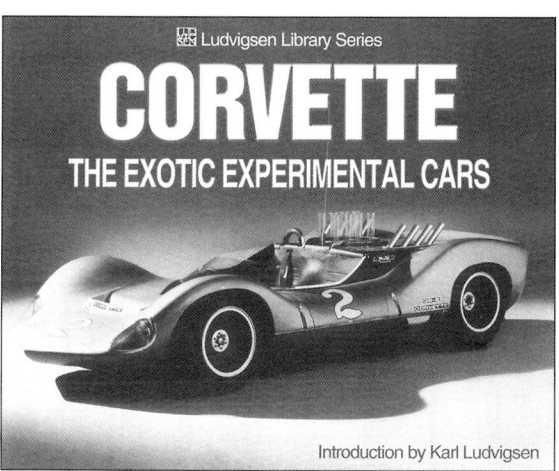

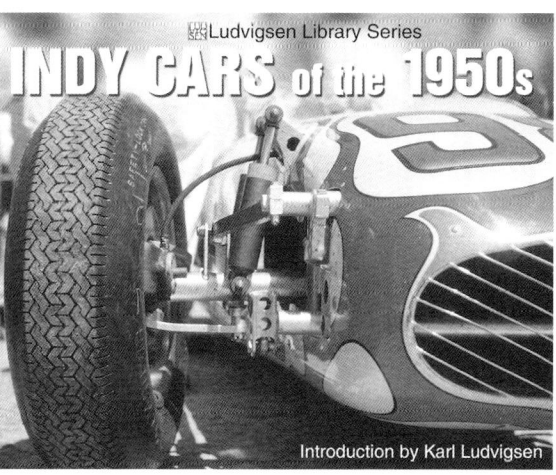
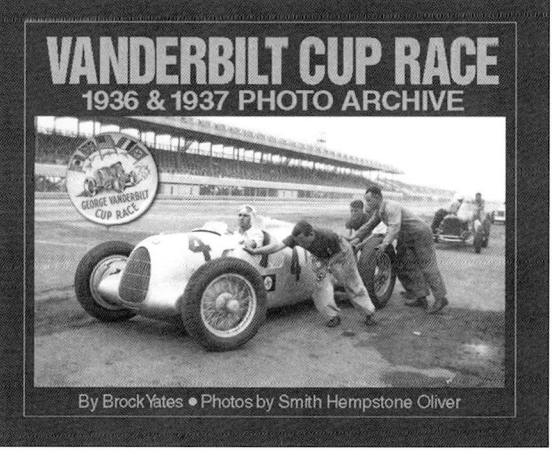

LUDVIGSEN LIBRARY LIMITED

The photographs in this book, supplied by the Ludvigsen Library, are available to purchase. Based in London, this extensive automotive library, founded and owned by Karl Ludvigsen, is one of the world's most comprehensive sources of reference material about cars and the motor industry. Specializing in car and motor racing photography, it includes much rare and unpublished original material from John Dugdale, Edward Eves, Max Le Grand, Peter Keen, Karl Ludvigsen, Rodolfo Mailander, Ove Nielsen, Stanley Rosenthall, and others.

All black and white prints are hand finished to museum display standards using the finest Ilford 1K fibre which gives a beautiful, durable finish that is perfect for mounting and display. Prints can be ordered from the Ludvigsen Library at the address below in three sizes at the following prices:

10 x 12	inches	US$40.00	UK£25.00
12 x 16	inches	US$55.00	UK£35.00
16 x 20	inches	US$75.00	UK£45.00

Please inquire concerning color, other sizes, and other subjects. Prices do not include packing and shipping fees, which will be advised in advance.

THE LUDVIGSEN LIBRARY LIMITED: 73 COLLIER STREET, LONDON N1 9BE, UNITED KINGDOM
TELEPHONE +44 (020) 7837 1700 FACSIMILE +44 (020) 7837 1776
E-MAIL LIBRARY@LUDVIGSEN.COM   HTTP://WWW.LUDVIGSEN.COM